DEADLINE

Also by Harry Reid:

Dear Country: A Quest for England

Outside Verdict: An Old Kirk in a New Scotland

The Final Whistle? Scottish Football, The Best and Worst of Times

DEADLINE
THE STORY OF THE SCOTTISH PRESS

HARRY REID

SAINT ANDREW PRESS
Edinburgh

First published in 2006 by
SAINT ANDREW PRESS
121 George Street, Edinburgh EH2 4YN

Copyright © Harry Reid, 2006
By arrangement with the BBC
The BBC logo is a trade mark of the British Broadcasting Corporation
and is used under licence
BBC logo © BBC 1996

Graphic designer of *Deadline* logo: Craig Caddis

10-digit ISBN 0 7152 0836 5 (paperback)
13-digit ISBN 978 0 7152 0836 6 (paperback)

British Library Cataloguing in Publication Data
A catalogue record for this book is available from the British Library.

Typeset by Waverley Typesetters
Printed and bound by Creative Print & Design, Wales

*This book is dedicated to the memory of Arnold Kemp,
a very good journalist and a very dear friend.*

Contents

Preface

This book was inspired by the makers of the six-part BBC Scotland television series *Deadline*, a celebration of the last fifty years or so of the Scottish press. Neil McDonald, executive producer of the series, says he has never known an industry peopled by such strong characters. Some of these characters feature in the series. But the *Deadline* team interviewed many more journalists past and present, and not all of this testimony can be shown, even in a series of six programmes. So, this book records some of the absorbing comments and memories that were not included in the programmes, and it tries to place some of the interviews and comments and recollections in the wider context of a Scotland that was rapidly changing politically, culturally and sociologically.

Thus, although this book is manifestly *not* the book of the series, it reflects many of the concerns and issues raised in the six programmes, and I hope it manages to develop one or two of them. It also, like the programmes, acts as a last hurrah for those who took part in what was undoubtedly a golden age of the Scottish press. So, there is a lot of nostalgia here. Journalists, even the most cynical and hard-bitten, do nostalgia like few others do. They take a sumptuous relish in retelling the gorgeous tales of the past, and in perhaps just embroidering a little bit here and there. And why not, if – like the man said, all those years ago – it points a moral or adorns a tale?

And, although the book does seek to present a portrait of a wonderful period in the long and chancy saga of Scottish journalism, it would be fanciful and absurd to say that the Scottish people and Scottish journalists somehow fell in love with each other. Yet Scots did have a voracious appetite for newspapers, and Scotland was frequently cited as the most competitive marketplace in the entire world. Without question, it was a given that Scots were both avid readers and producers of newspapers.

That being the case, I find it surprising that there is no proper Museum of Scottish Journalism. I think that such a museum should exist, and furthermore I think that it should exist in Glasgow, which may have been the second city of the empire but was, for many, the first city of journalism. All of Scotland was involved in this peculiar, intense and tempestuous relationship with newspapers, but in Glasgow the relationship reached fever pitch. Indeed, I hope that the many hours of interview, now on film, will one day be handed over by the BBC to a Museum of Scottish Journalism, in the happy event of such an institution eventually becoming a reality.

Meanwhile, it is important to make clear that this book is mainly about daily newspaper journalism. There is relatively little in it about the Sunday press, or the weekly and bi-weekly press. It is tilted towards writing journalists, and there is not too much in these pages about production journalists or photographers, or for that matter about the many others who helped to produce and distribute newspapers, from copy boys to Linotype operators and upmakers, from circulation reps to van-drivers, from machine-minders to advertising salespeople, from wireroom operators to marketing executives. You could say that it presents a slightly skewed view of the press; and I would not demur. It is a personal and relentlessly subjective book. But it does, I hope, discuss some of the achievements and failures of the Scottish press in a manner that is both thoughtful and readable.

I am not a particularly convivial person, but it is impossible to survive as a Scottish journalist – particularly in Glasgow – without learning how to be convivial, without regarding the pub as just as important as the office. Indeed, one eminent Glasgow journalist is quoted in this book as saying that the pub *was* the office. I am strongly and sentimentally grateful for the camaraderie and friendship I have known in this always febrile and frequently crazy world of Scottish journalism. For all its faults and silliness, many seriously impressive if short-lived and instantly perishable products were produced night after night after night, always against the clock and always reflecting the honed and polished fruits of much intense and occasionally distinguished human endeavour.

Finally, I have to note that, in recent years, I have had the unfortunate task of delivering eulogies at the funerals of two men called Kemp. They were not related, though both worked on the *Scotsman* during its golden years, described elsewhere in this book. Willie Kemp, the *Scotsman*'s first-ever sports editor, was one of the journalists who took me in hand and gave me those informal lessons that mean so much more than any amount of theory and classroom or lecture-hall teaching. Even more important to me was the second man called Kemp.

This man, Arnold, also taught me much. He had ink in his blood. He grew up in the Canonmills area of north Edinburgh. At the end of his street was the Northern Bar, where print workers who produced the Scottish edition of the *Daily Mail* at the Tanfield works drank and blethered and occasionally caroused. From a young age, Arnold started doing odd jobs at the Tanfield plant. He was fascinated by the buzz, the shabby glamour, the forlorn effort. (He once told me that a big Buick was hired to transport early editions through to Glasgow to compete for street sales with the *Scottish Daily Express*, then in its pomp. He reckoned that everyone was aware of the futility of the gesture, yet somehow they still believed in it.)

After serving the *Scotsman* for almost twenty years, he went on to become an eminent editor of the *Herald* – probably its best editor of the twentieth century. Arnold Kemp was not only a constantly blithe and brilliant colleague but also a very dear friend. This book is dedicated to his memory.

Note: Chapters 1 and 3 cover some of the same events, but from different perspectives. The Scottish press's virtual invention – and consequent promotion – of devolution as a major political issue is a key recurring theme in the book and is treated in various chapters, as is the – so far – disappointing outcome.

HARRY REID
Edinburgh

Introduction

The long, sometimes heroic, often impertinent, usually breathless and – for the most part – honourable saga of the Scottish press probably began in earnest 345 years ago with the publication of the first Scottish newspaper, the *Mercurius Scoticus*. Published in Leith, and as obscure as its title, it didn't last long; it was launched in 1651 and died the next year. Before then, indeed ever since the invention of the printing press, there had been various news sheets, usually even more short-lived than the *Mercurius* – but whether or not they could be dignified, if that is the appropriate term, with the appellation of newspaper is another matter.

Far more significant than the *Mercurius* was the *Aberdeen Journal*. It was launched in 1748 and was the venerable parent paper of what is now the *Aberdeen Press and Journal*. The *Press and Journal* occupies the proud slot of number two in the list of the world's oldest surviving daily newspapers. This broadsheet, consistently parochial but consistently thorough and reliable in its news coverage of the North-East and the Highlands and Islands, is a Scottish newspaper that has often been underestimated. At the end of 2005, it was selling more than 85,000 copies a day, considerably more than either the *Scotsman* or the *Herald*.

Eighth on that list of the world's oldest daily papers is the *Herald*, until 1992 the *Glasgow Herald*, which first appeared in 1783. Its first scoop was perhaps the most spectacular in its long and generally illustrious history – early hard news of American independence. Its founder, publisher, printer and editor, one John Mennons, was putting his first edition together when he received, by happy coincidence, a communication from the Lord Provost of Glasgow. It was a copy of a letter the Provost had just received from the Foreign Secretary, giving early news of the Treaty of Versailles, which guaranteed American independence. Mennons was not over-excited by the news; he placed it on the back page.

The *Glasgow Herald* was to play a key role in establishing Glasgow as Scotland's media capital, a role it retains to this day despite the siting of the new Scottish Parliament in the capital city, Edinburgh, forty-five miles to the east. Since the *Herald* was born in 1783, more than 150 newspapers have been founded in Glasgow. Sadly, apart from the *Herald*, only four survive: the *Evening Times*, the *Daily Record*, the *Sunday Mail* and the *Sunday Herald*. And the *Sunday Herald* is very much an infant, having been born as recently as 1999.

A fifth paper, the *Scottish Daily Express*, launched in Glasgow in 1928, still exists – but only as a Scottish edition of the English *Express*. It is a pale shadow of the *Scottish Daily Express* in its pomp, a paper that was aggressively Scottish, with a swashbuckling sense of its own Caledonian importance, a Scottish paper that in the 1960s employed over twenty feature-writers and over thirty sportswriters.

It was in the mid-1800s that the Scottish press, like its English counterpart, began to take shape in the form we all know, and some of us love, today. The abolition of the tax on advertisements, quickly followed by the repeal of stamp duty, created a fresh commercial impetus for both existing and new journals. And newspapers that had hitherto usually been little more than crude squibs became much more considered and educative, if still very partisan in their political coverage.

This process reflected not just a new commercial freedom but also a considerable increase in literacy.

The heady heyday of the Scottish press lasted for most of the twentieth century. The years from about 1950 until the end of the century were extra special, and this book is mainly about them.

Scots devoured newspapers with a relish that was unparalleled anywhere else. Many households took in two, three or even more daily papers; queues were frequently seen outside newsagents' shops. Many local papers were published. About 200 of them still exist. These papers, usually weekly or bi-weekly, are often read more avidly than their national counterparts.

❛❜

Scotland produced several generations of fine journalists. The press rapidly acquired a powerful social influence, as could be seen in the way that Scottish newspapers enthusiastically and effectively encouraged recruitment for the military in the early days of the First World War. Two pan-Scotland papers, the *Scottish Daily Express* and the *Daily Record*, eventually had, in the late 1960s, a combined circulation of well over a million – in a country with a population of barely five million.

Those were days when, more than now, the readers appreciated their newspapers, identified with them and took pride in them. And the people who produced these papers regarded themselves as special. If that sounds cocky – well, cockiness was part of the game. Scottish journalism was full of bravado, mischief and mystique; you could cover a story about a noxious and malodorous smell emanating from a derelict pit bing, as I once did, and still sincerely feel that there was something glamorous and exciting about what you were doing.

There was an underlying sense of purpose that somehow managed to be earnest and cheeky at the same time. Journalists were very cynical, yet they were also romantics, and at least some of them genuinely believed that from time to time they were informing and entertaining the Scottish public – and maybe even educating it a little, too.

Mingled with this sense of purpose was arrogance, and also conceit. The finest football writer I knew, the *Scotsman's* John Rafferty, used to tell me in all seriousness: 'It's not true till I write it'. I once covered a story with a squad of three from the *Scottish Daily Express*: reporter, photographer and 'driver' – this last being the muscle. I actually heard the immortal words, as we walked through the factory gates (it was an industrial dispute): 'This is the *Scottish Daily Express*, and we're moving in'. This portentous announcement was intoned by the 'driver' without a trace of irony. Whatever the context – and some of the contexts were pretty drab and mean – there was, absurd as it may seem in retrospect, a palpable sense of adventure.

There are many old-timers still around: elderly, affable codgers who can talk well and can recount heroic and not-so-heroic exploits. These exploits were often but not invariably drink-fuelled, and always had the great aims, in descending order of importance, of pleasing or at least appeasing that grizzled tyrant the news editor, beating the opposition and perhaps, as a remote afterthought, informing the readers. I think the witness of these men (they were mostly men; the female journalists were a special and in many ways brave and distinguished minority – very much a minority) is important for all sorts of reasons – historical, sociological, cultural.

There remain just a few who can recall when pigeons were a customary method of getting the news back to headquarters. There are more around who can remember the extraordinary days of hot metal. But even that generation will not last forever, though some of them seem to think that they will. The stories and the memories of these good folk are important and worth recording. The BBC Scotland series *Deadline* gives some of them a chance to reminisce to a wide audience, and that is important. It is, to use an old journalistic phrase, history shot on the wing.

❝ ❞

Now, in the early years of the twenty-first century, the picture is darker and more problematic. Newspapers face challenges which were unimagined even a generation ago. I wrote the above paragraphs on an early spring morning in Scotland's capital city. At about 8:15am, I left my keyboard and wandered along to the local newsagent; this is my morning routine. I buy a paper for myself, another for my wife, and, if I am in expansive mood, a third for luck.

Most mornings, I have a brief chat with the agent, a genial and perceptive Italian gentleman in his early fifties who has owned his shop for more than twenty-five years. He monitors, in his subjective and directly interested way, the decline of the Scottish press, and he regularly mentions to me that fewer and fewer people are buying newspapers in his shop (which is nonetheless always busy). Even cigarette sales seem to be holding up better. When he started, there were no supermarkets in the vicinity; now there are several. He suspects, probably validly, that his newspaper supplier gives them priority treatment. But that is a technicality; his main fear for newspapers is that they are no longer a particularly popular product.

His business is situated at a busy crossroads where two major commuter arteries meet. Around his shop are many tenement flats, with a largely transient population. He notes that it is the older, longer-established local residents – generally those who live in houses rather than flats – who still buy newspapers. To put it bluntly, these customers are slowly dying off, and are not being replaced by new newspaper-buyers. He often complains that young people hardly ever purchase a newspaper.

As I returned home that morning, reflecting on this gloomy mantra, I walked past three buses queuing at the traffic lights. In each, I could see a few passengers reading papers – but every single one of them was reading the *Metro*, the successful free tabloid produced by Associated Newspapers that has been taken up with enthusiasm by Scotland's commuters. When I returned to my computer, I could, if I had wished, have gone online and summoned up newspapers, stories and information (and misinformation) from all over the globe. Or I could have switched on the television and looked through the many satellite and digital news channels on offer, again from all over the world. Universal information, instant access, colossal choice – printed newspapers suddenly seem to be a rather tired mode of communication.

Yet I am not a pessimist. I think that too many older journalists (and newsagents) assume that their industry is dying. Obituaries of the newspaper have often been written, and have always proved to be premature. The times are hard for the Scottish newspaper industry, but there is no need to repine. The Scottish press will, as it often has in the past, regroup and reinvent itself. The vast and incredibly impressive circulations of the past may be gone forever; but, even in this era of rapidly declining readerships, the circulation performance of the Scottish press is remarkable.

This book is mainly about the recent past, not the future. It is imbued with nostalgia; but, as I have tried to suggest, it is nostalgia with a historical significance. Scotland's love affair with newspapers was phenomenal, and the Scottish journalist was a phenomenon – sometimes glorious, sometimes pathetic, but almost always wondrous to behold.

1

A Quintet of Editors

This chapter is both a personal meditation on editor-ship and an informal memoir of the five editors, all very different, for whom I have worked. The first was Sir Alastair Dunnett, who had edited the *Daily Record* with both showmanship and a well-disguised seriousness for almost a decade when Roy Thomson, the new proprietor of the *Scotsman*, enticed him through to the east in 1955.

Thomson was a brash, dynamic and fabulously wealthy Canadian entrepreneur who had acquired the *Scotsman* cheaply and in so doing had infuriated the more snooty elements in the paper's readership. He compounded matters by appointing as his new editor a supposedly downmarket journalist from Glasgow. This snobbishness may seem, in retrospect, utterly ridiculous. But the *Scotsman* has always had an uneasy relationship with its home city. Glasgow's relationship with the *Herald* has, for the most part, been closer and fonder.

The Edinburgh establishment met its match in Dunnett. He had a wonderful way with words. When he felt the need to obfuscate or divert, he could deploy a peculiar Celtic whimsy; the words sounded good, even if they turned out to be meaningless. He was adept at public relations, and, in his slightly wheezy way, he was a superb raconteur. The phrase 'gift of the gab' could have been invented for him.

Early on in Dunnett's time at the *Scotsman*, a mid-ranking journalist sought an audience with the great man, seeking a pay rise. After twenty minutes listening to Dunnett, he emerged to remark ruefully that he had gained not a penny on his salary, but he was at least convinced of the need for a Forth Road Bridge. A superb promoter of his paper, and of himself, Dunnett had an even greater talent: spotting it in others. And not only could he spot talent, he was also prepared to back his hunches. He plucked from the ranks, to use his own phrase, a hard-working Aberdonian sub-editor called Eric Mackay.

Mackay was appointed London editor of the paper in 1957; he returned to Edinburgh in 1961 and rapidly became *de facto* editor. Dunnett, always gregarious, now had an excellent production man in place to run the paper each night. He could devote himself to his ambassadorial duties, literally across the globe; he travelled the world addressing Caledonian Societies and the like. But he never totally neglected Edinburgh, and he carefully wooed the city's various elites while zealously protecting his paper's integrity. Meanwhile, Mackay got on with producing the paper.

Perhaps Dunnett's most unlikely appointment came early in his long editorship when he appointed not a journalist, but rather an unassuming sports enthusiast from the caseroom, as the paper's first sports editor. This modest man, Willie Kemp, was one of the great unsung heroes of Scottish journalism in the 1950s and 1960s. He presided over some of the finest sportswriting that has ever appeared in the Scottish press. Dunnett and Kemp between them ensured that the paper took football, Scotland's premier sport, seriously. Two great – and the word is used advisedly – football writers were hired from the west: first Hugh McIlvanney and then, when the *Observer* tempted Hugh south, John Rafferty, who had been a teacher in Glasgow. (Rafferty came to journalism very late, and was quite a few years older than the man he succeeded.) Dunnett and Kemp also appointed Norman Mair, a gloriously eccentric but exceptionally well-informed writer who had represented Scotland at both rugby and cricket – though his own favourite sport was golf.

Here was the *Scotsman* signalling that it took sport seriously. In those staid days, this was no mean breakthrough. In Glasgow, the *Herald* was maintaining a pompous and stuffy reserve when it came to the raffish and vulgar world of professional sport – so much so that the editor of the paper, James Holburn, thought that the main sporting event of each year occurred every September, when the new captain of the Royal and Ancient at St Andrews drove himself into office at the hangman's hour of 8am. (I have this on the authority of the *Herald*'s then football and golf correspondent, Raymond Jacobs.)

Incredibly, the *Glasgow Herald* did not deem it necessary to send Raymond to Lisbon in May 1967, when Celtic were playing in the European Cup final. When that superlative team, managed by Jock Stein and inspired by the likes of Jimmy Johnstone, Bobby Murdoch, Billy McNeill and Tommy Gemmell, became the first British club to win the European Cup, the *Glasgow Herald* – to its eternal shame – was absent. The correspondent of the *Evening Times* had been asked to file a match report from Lisbon for the *Herald*, its sister paper.

Much later, Raymond Jacobs told me that he had considered resigning. I asked Raymond if there might have been an undercurrent of sectarianism in the extraordinary snubbing of Celtic; at the time, a certain faint pall of anti-Catholicism hung over the *Herald*'s premises in Mitchell Street. But Raymond said no, he was convinced that the decision simply reflected the paper's Olympian disdain for professional sport in general and football in particular.

The point of this is not so much to indict the aloof short-sightedness of the *Glasgow Herald*, though that was deplorable, as to commend the foresight and acumen of Dunnett. John Rafferty was, as it happened, a Celtic supporter, and his writing about the Glasgow team's exploits in the late 1960s was constantly ecstatic. But well might it have been; that Celtic team was by far the finest club side Scotland has ever produced.

Now that sports journalism has become so pervasive, it is salutary to look back on those years. When I was working as a news sub-editor on the *Scotsman* in 1970, I would, when I finished my shift, walk over to the sports desk, which was undermanned and overstretched, and help with the second-edition changes. This appalled some of my more senior news sub-editing colleagues, not because they thought I was over-eager, but rather because they thought I was demeaning myself – and, by implication, them – by choosing voluntarily to soil my hands with sports copy. One of them once said to me, in all seriousness: 'Slumming again tonight, Harry?'

❛❜

Another inspired Dunnett appointment was the young Arnold Kemp, whom Dunnett hired as a sub-editor when, by Arnold's own account, he was a somewhat gauche and underachieving Edinburgh University graduate whose one ambition was to work for newspapers. Dunnett took a chance with him, and he went on to become, for many, the finest Scottish journalist of his generation. Other significant Dunnett appointments were Magnus Magnusson, who was to become the most high-profile of all Scottish journalists of the past generation or so, and Gus Macdonald and Arnold's brother David – all of whom went on to distinguished careers in television journalism. The three of them at one point formed a rather wild investigative unit called Close Up. Here, as in so much, Dunnett was ahead of his time.

Dunnett was an astute but increasingly remote editor. He enjoyed the total confidence of his owner Roy Thomson, who also entrusted Dunnett with all aspects of the management not just of the paper, but of the whole business. For several years, Dunnett combined editing the *Scotsman* with the role of managing director of Scotsman Publications, and was thus responsible for the overall running of both the *Scotsman* and the *Evening News*. Such an arrangement would be unheard of today. The demarcation between editorial and management is now guarded jealously, and even a flamboyant showman like Dunnett, at once canny and inspirational, could not straddle it.

❛ ❜

Eric Mackay hired me in 1969. Then in his late forties, Mackay was effectively in charge of the paper, and he made that clear in the interview, though I recall that we spent most of the time talking about the decline of Aberdeen Football Club. When I reappeared a month or so later to start work in the *Scotsman*'s grandiose offices on North Bridge, Edinburgh, I was ushered into the presence of Dunnett along with two other graduate recruits, Colm Brogan and David Leigh. Dunnett gave us a rambling pep talk that we could not understand; somewhat earnestly, we went over what he had said in the pub later, and were still none the wiser. It was like a rather fatuous homily. I remember that his remarks featured the filthy state of the Scott Monument, which Dunnett could gaze at from the window of his editorial office on the few occasions he was there. We could not work out whether this was intended as a subtle commentary on the wider condition of Edinburgh or indeed of Scotland. Then the three of us were packed off to train in Newcastle, a harder school where such fanciful whimsy would have been scorned mercilessly.

When we returned, almost a year later, I started work as a sub-editor, reporting for duty at 4:30 each afternoon. I was not working in an exciting or glamorous environment. Most of the sub-editors were middle-aged, and the rest were elderly. There was not a single woman present. Many of the subs wore stained cardigans. Only one of them, a splendidly erudite and irascible Irishman called Gaffney, had a reputation for drinking; his cardigan was beer-stained. Most of the men drank disgusting coffee that they kept in battered flasks. Gaffney had various hiding places where he stored bottles of Guinness.

With the possible exception of the volatile Gaffney, there was a pervasive dreariness about my new colleagues. I remember observing one of the subs arriving for work and spending a good ten minutes removing his pencils from his pencil case and then sharpening them, one by one. (These were very much days of old technology.) When he had at last arranged them to his satisfaction in a neat row, he walked, in solemn and stately fashion, up to the copytaster's desk to receive his first copy of the evening. This sub was reputed to have once struggled for more than an hour to find a heading for a brief story about the death of an old Edinburgh worthy, a former councillor. He eventually came up with the two words: 'Octogenarian succumbs'.

These subs were poorly paid but well-educated men; they had a vast store of eclectic knowledge. They worked with care and pedantic precision. There was nothing slapdash about them; but nor was there any flair or verve. They carried an air of dignified defeat. If you did not fancy the appalling liquid that oozed from their flasks, you could summon a copy boy who would fetch you some tepid so-called coffee from the battered, filthy old machine in the far corner of the newsroom. Occasional shouts for a copy boy were just about the only sounds to breach the somnolent silence. I sometimes yelled for a boy not so much because I wanted more bad coffee but simply because I had a desperate need to smash the doom-laden silence.

I describe all this to indicate that, despite Dunnett's deserved reputation for innovation, and the sleek and lively persona that he cultivated, the *Scotsman* was not produced in a manner that mirrored his style. Although the comment and business and features and sports and arts pages were all being developed to good effect, the news pages remained dull and dreary, reflecting the environment in which they were produced.

The paradox was that the man who was to preside over the much-needed livening-up process was a much more introverted figure than Dunnett. This was Eric Mackay. Fast-forward say five years into Mackay's editorship, and everything was transformed. There was a buzz about the entire newsroom. And there were actually a few women present.

❛❜

While I was on those early shifts with the news subs, I noted that, each evening, Mackay, who was still deputy editor, would quietly materialise in the big newsroom and would sit on the backbench beside the chief sub-editor and the production editor for an hour or so as the paper was taking shape. He would occasionally wander around the newsroom, having a quiet word here and a quiet word there. He always appeared without a jacket, with his sleeves rolled up, as if he meant business. I never once saw Dunnett with his jacket off.

But then, Dunnett was rarely to be seen. One evening, he suddenly appeared, dapper as ever, in an astrakhan coat, carrying a large suitcase. It seemed to be heavy, and he placed it with difficulty on the desk next to mine, gave a cursory nod in my direction, opened it, fished around among what appeared to be cashmere garments of some kind and eventually produced a pile of grubby-looking documents. He then took these up to the chief sub-editor, came back, closed the case and vanished. The sub-editor opposite me had been with the paper for three years. 'Who on earth was that?' he asked.

Early in 1972, Dunnett's friend, protector and mentor Roy Thomson appointed him supremo of his nascent North Sea oil interests. This was Mackay's chance for the editor's chair; but, for some time, the North Bridge gossip machine had decreed that he and Dunnett were falling out. By this time, I was attending the occasional editorial conference, and I had noted the insouciant, even dismissive attitude that Mackay adopted when Dunnett launched into one of his elaborate tales. Once, to my amazement, Mackay actually started whistling softly and gazing pointedly at the ceiling as Dunnett meandered through an interminable story about a Highland stationmaster.

By now, the hot tip for the next editor was not Mackay but Alastair Stuart, the paper's London editor. However, Mackay got the job, and in his modest self-effacing way – he was laconic to the point of dourness – he emerged as a great editor. It was soon apparent that he was around, constantly. For the first time, I became directly aware of how important and influential an editor is, or should be.

❛ ❜

Dunnett was without doubt a man of vision. His contribution to the intellectual and cultural life of modern Scotland should not be underestimated. For example, he built up in the *Scotsman* a formidable leader-writing team, consisting of Matt Moulton, J. D. Vassie, Andrew Hood and Willis Pickard. This made the *Scotsman* an intellectual powerhouse. Dunnett encouraged them to develop the paper's policy on devolution, a political concept that was hardly heard of in the mid-1960s. Andrew Hood, a key member of the leader-writing team who also took on the job of letters editor, reckons that it was after Winnie Ewing's spectacular success for the SNP in the Hamilton by-election of 1967 that Dunnett began to think seriously about constitutional change.

In 1968, a series of exceptionally prescient editorials in the *Scotsman* in effect kicked off the home-rule campaign that many years later bore fruit with the arrival of the new Scottish Parliament in 1999. These leaders created such interest that they were republished in booklet form. In the following year, the prime minister, Harold Wilson, appointed a commission under Lord Crowther to examine whether there was a need for constitutional change. Wilson was a cynical operator, and he sometimes set up Royal Commissions as a means of kicking a tricky problem into the long grass. With a bit of luck, the commission would not report for several years. (It was once suggested, seriously, that he should set up a Royal Commission on Royal Commissions.) Whatever Wilson's motives, the fact that Crowther and his colleagues interviewed leading members of the great and the good as to their view on devolution helped to give the notion credibility.

Sadly, Crowther died before his work was completed. His place was taken by Lord Kilbrandon, whose commission's report was at last published at the end of 1973. It recommended directly elected Scottish and Welsh assemblies.

❝❞

Dunnett appointed an arts editor, Allen Wright, a man he 'plucked', to use one of his favourite words again, from the *Scotsman* news desk. Although Allen was not the most perspicacious critic himself – he often told the story of how he attended the Edinburgh Fringe première of *Rosencrantz and Guildenstern Are Dead* and opined that Tom Stoppard would never make a playwright – he was a superb organiser. With hardly any assistance, he built the *Scotsman's* coverage of the Edinburgh Festival, and particularly the Festival Fringe, into something that was awesome in its scope and authority. Allen worked longer hours than any other journalist I have come across. At one stage, when I was a feature-writer, I had a craze for writing my stories very early in the morning – the cleaners vacated the features room at about seven, and I would appear about then. Allen was often in before me. And I knew he'd be there at midnight, checking the late theatre and concert reviews.

Even more central to the *Scotsman's* growing reputation for intelligent and comprehensive coverage of the burgeoning Scottish arts scene was Dunnett's appointment of Conrad Wilson. It was in 1962, when Wilson was working for the BBC in London, that Dunnett appointed him to the paper's London staff; two years later, he became the *Scotsman's* full-time music critic. This was a bold appointment.

Wilson was a fearless and relentlessly controversial writer, sometimes appearing to go out of his way to infuriate the paper's bourgeois readers. Looking back on his early days, Wilson says: 'Yes, I was outspoken. I smashed things up. I had total contempt for safe stuff like the annual *Messiah* at the Usher Hall. I championed composers like Peter Maxwell Davies and Harry Birtwhistle, who were anathema to the paper's more staid concert-goers. Dunnett was enormously and consistently supportive. He repelled people who came to see him to demand that I should be fired. My great enemy was Professor Sidney Newman, who had the chair of music at Edinburgh University. More than once, he explicitly told Dunnett that I must be sacked. What you might call the Edinburgh musical establishment put Dunnett under severe pressure, but the man never flinched. He backed me all the way.'

Dunnett cherished the Edinburgh Festival, and he was proud of the *Scotsman's* considerable contribution to the Festival's growing status. Yet, paradoxically, despite his commendable support for Conrad Wilson and his sympathy for the avant-garde, when it came to the performing arts, he was at heart an establishment man. We only once had a row, and that was shortly before he left the paper. During one of his rare appearances, I told him that I was keen to do a feature on what I thought was the excessive public subsidy being given to opera in Scotland. Dunnett was, for once, brusque. He flatly said he would have none of it. When I tried to argue with him, he shouted: 'The matter is closed!'

Dunnett was a courageous and even prophetic editor. The flaw in him was that, increasingly, his paper did not benefit from his flamboyant persona and his far-sighted instincts. He was latterly an absentee editor – and absentee editors are not good editors. (Looking back at Dunnett's regime, I have, I hope, made it clear that I had relatively little direct experience of his editorial style. He is due respect; he revived the *Scotsman* and was in many ways ahead of his time. Much of what I have written above is based on conversations I had over the years with the two – unrelated – Kemps, Willie and Arnold, and also with Andrew Hood, who joined the *Scotsman* in 1961. I only worked for Dunnett during the last, coda period of his editorship, and I hardly knew him. The other four editors for whom I worked I got to know well.)

( )

Eric Mackay presided over a great era on the *Scotsman*. I am biased. As I progressed through various jobs, from reporter to sportswriter to feature-writer to education correspondent to features editor, I was increasingly aware that Mackay, and his deputy Arnold Kemp, had not just assembled a fine team of journalists but had also, more importantly, given the paper cohesion, editorial momentum and a terrific sense of common purpose. Partly, this was because Mackay had inherited Dunnett's prescient commitment to home rule, and he developed it with even more enthusiasm. Indeed, the *Scotsman* campaigned for constitutional change with such zeal that it was validly criticised for being a one-issue paper, and some critics even alleged – wrongly, I believe – that the commitment to home rule was so strong that the demarcation between reporting and comment was sometimes fudged.

Mackay's only pal on the paper was John Rafferty, the football writer. As an editor, he stayed aloof socially; he never came into the two great *Scotsman* pubs (the Jinglin' Geordie and the Halfway House) in Fleshmarket Close, the infamous alley behind the building. He left that kind of socialising to his endlessly genial deputy, Arnold Kemp.

Mackay was a man with a mission. Not only was he intensely committed to Dunnett's editorial policy of devolution; he also took to saying that he wished to 'unite Scotland'. Although he assembled a team of articulate and fluent journalists, he was himself by no means a natural communicator, and we were not always sure exactly what this mantra about uniting Scotland entailed, although we reckoned that the putative Scottish Assembly would, when it arrived, pull Scotland together.

But would it? We were careless of our wider consistuency; we were so caught up in pursuing what seemed to some outsiders to be nothing less than a crusade that we forgot there were many sceptics among the readership – including many of those outside the central belt, within the business community, many of the older readers, and so on. Yet the *Scotsman* had found a cause, and it pursued it with spirit and aggression. The paper was on a roll. And a good proportion of the readers did appreciate what they were receiving. New readers were coming on board. When Mackay took over from Dunnett in 1972, the paper's circulation was just under 75,000. The circulation rose steadily, if not spectacularly, and by 1979 it had almost reached the talismanic target of 100,000.

There was no doubt an element of self-interest in Mackay's commitment to devolution. The Assembly would be situated in Edinburgh – and the *Scotsman*, having led the campaign for it, would be in pole position to report its proceedings. Mackay, although his own politics tended to be Liberal, was appointed by the Labour government of the mid-1970s as executive chairman of a committee to plan all the media dispositions for the proposed Assembly – for example, would there be a lobby, on the Westminster model? (Mackay was personally very much against this.) Occasionally, he would travel to London for discussions with Cabinet ministers about the mechanics of constitutional change.

Mackay was quietly but firmly building both the *Scotsman's* status and its influence. His masterstroke involved the hiring not of a career journalist but of a brilliant if abrasive academic. John P. Mackintosh, a professor of politics and the Labour MP for East Lothian, was given a Monday column. His erudite, pungent and forceful offerings contained the most cerebrally impressive writing I have ever come across in Scottish, indeed British, journalism. Mackintosh was an expert on the British constitution and had written a Penguin special edition on devolution. He, more than anyone, led the intellectual charge.

The eminent Scottish journalist George Rosie returned to Scotland from London in 1975 to become the first Scottish-affairs correspondent of the *Sunday Times*. He recalls: 'Devolution was *the* story then, and I researched it carefully. It was clear to me that, if the *Scotsman* didn't actually invent it, they pretty well did. In the mid- and late 1970s, they kind of exploited the devolution debate; they covered it with a lot of energy, with some really sharp writing.'

The sharpest of all these writers was not a staff journalist but Mackintosh, the politician/academic. It is significant that Mackintosh was a Labour politician. Some critics of the *Scotsman* at this time suggested that the paper was infested by nationalists; but, apart from the leader-writer Colin Bell, I cannot recall any senior journalist on the paper who was a card-carrying member of the party. Indeed, the Nats, who had eleven MPs at Westminster and were growing in importance, were often extremely critical of the *Scotsman* for not being nationalist enough.

Stuart Trotter, who was at that time working in the Palace of Westminster for the *Glasgow Herald*, and went on to be chairman of the Press Gallery, recalls those years: 'The *Scotsman* took the many constitutional debates very seriously indeed, and covered them in enormous detail. But the paradox was that the paper's team at Westminster – David Bradford, Tom James and George Jones (who went on to become political editor of the *Daily Telegraph*) – were not quite so enthused by the devolution cause.'

Trotter reckons that one of the reasons the Labour Party finally took up devolution enthusiastically in the 1970s was because of its fear of the SNP. 'Many Labour politicians became seriously scared of the Nats, and afraid of the possibility of independence. So they changed their minds about constitutional change. They came to see devolution as the best way to prevent independence.' Trotter also remembers that, in the 1970s, Scottish affairs suddenly became the talk of Westminster. 'Many London-based journalists had not taken Scotland at all seriously. Now all sorts of people, members of the Press Gallery, English MPs, even journalists from abroad, were starting to ask all sorts of questions about Scotland.'

Arnold Kemp, the *Scotsman's* deputy editor, was hostile to the Nats. Neal Ascherson, the leading writer on Scottish politics, was a high-minded Old Etonian with something of a disdain for the smoke-filled rooms that were the customary political habitat of the times, though he did play a role in the founding of the Scottish Labour Party in 1975 along with various other free spirits of the left such as the politicians Jim Sillars and John Robertson, the journalists John Pirie and Bob Brown, and the educationist Bob Tait.

The specific constituencies that were being neglected by the Scottish press were Unionism and business. You would have expected the *Glasgow Herald* to speak up for them – and it tried to do so, but in a dull, half-hearted way. In truth, the *Herald* was in the doldrums. Not even the appointment of a new and lively editor, Iain Lindsay Smith, in the mid-1970s, managed to revive it. George Rosie recalls: 'The *Herald* was flagging very badly. It didn't enjoy the great debate on devolution. It was listless.'

Mackay and the *Scotsman* had seized the high intellectual ground, and there was not another editor or paper around to provide a challenge. The *Scottish Daily Express* – right-wing, belligerent and full of chutzpah – might well have done so in its glory days, but it had been brought down by union militants. So, the *Scotsman's* quest for devolution became the talk of Westminster, and even Europe; many European journalists visited North Bridge to be briefed by the likes of Ascherson or Kemp. The atmosphere on the paper was purposeful and heady. Ascherson was impressed by Eric Mackay's fervent belief that devolution would lead to a serious moral and political recovery in Scottish life. George Rosie goes so far as to say: 'Eric Mackay did far more than any other journalist to create the Scotland we live in today'.

When I joined the *Scotsman* in 1969, I assumed that after five or six years I would move on to London and try my luck there. I stayed on at the *Scotsman* because it was, in the 1970s, a very happy paper – and also because Mackay had somehow made us convinced that Scotland was the only place to be. The downside was that the *Scotsman* was in danger of becoming obsessed – never a happy state for a newspaper. It all ended in tears, as I shall explain.

❛ ❜

After he had been editor for about a year, Mackay totally transformed the paper's approach to newsgathering by appointing a new group of specialist writers to write about areas which had previously been covered by diary reporters in the newsroom. Among the six or seven appointed were Neal Ascherson to cover Scottish national politics, David Scott to cover local politics, Frank Frazer to cover energy (crucially important at this time, as the North Sea oil boom was under way and there was a growing debate about nuclear power) and myself to cover education.

This was a bold move by Mackay. He encountered some resistance from two of his stalwarts, the news editor Stuart Brown and Stuart's deputy John Hepburn. There were mischievous suggestions that the new specialist team was to be a sort of elite cadre, though Mackay did not see it that way. Up until then, the key – in some cases the only – high-profile specialists on Scottish papers had been the industrial correspondents, influential figures like Ian Imrie on the *Glasgow Herald* and Jack McGill on the *Scottish Daily Express*. Sadly, they had essentially been the chroniclers of decline, covering the running-down of Scotland's old industrial base and the closures of shipyards, car factories and the like.

The exception was the *Daily Record*, then being edited with flair and authority by the eccentric and underestimated Bernie Vickers. He had the foresight to create a small but effective team of specialists, including Harry Conroy on finance and property, Stewart McLaughlan on Scottish politics and John Pirie on education. John was to become a good friend of mine, and taught me much about journalism. Indeed, this friendship and tutelage was perhaps the biggest bonus I had during my four years as an education specialist.

I was reluctant to become the *Scotsman's* first education correspondent; but Mackay, in – for him – a very long pep talk, explained to me that the job would be invaluable for me as well as good for the paper. He said that I would learn how Scotland worked. And he was right: I learned much about the Scottish Office, and its relations with Westminster, and about the interface between central and local government. I also learned a lot about industrial relations because, at that time there was a growing mood of militancy among Scottish teachers, and also among students and university lecturers. Scotland's largest union, the Educational Institute of Scotland, which had been a rather staid and pseudo-academic organisation, was transformed almost overnight by John Pollock, its charismatic new general secretary, a barnstorming figure who had been a reforming secondary-school head in Ayrshire.

At that time, a small group of politically motivated militants had infiltrated the union, and John Pollock's method of regaining control was to embrace militancy himself. Given the teachers' appalling salaries and conditions, this was easily achieved, and the union was transformed into a fighting machine. The smaller teaching unions had to follow suit. By the end of 1974, most Scottish teachers were out on strike in the first of three great set-piece bouts of industrial action which were to afflict Scottish primary and secondary education in the 1970s and 1980s.

At the same time, the (then) eight Scottish universities were alarmed by the devolution proposals which the Labour government, egged on by the *Scotsman*, was drafting, and insisted rather shrilly that they had to be allowed to stay outside the devolution settlement. Covering this gave me new insights into the nature of powerbroking at a high level – not a particularly edifying education, but a useful one. As noted, I was reluctant to take on the job of education correspondent; but in retrospect I am highly grateful to Mackay for his foresight and his good sense.

The great pan-Scotland tabloid, the *Record*, had in John Pirie a specialist who was well equipped to deal with the volatile educational scene. The *Glasgow Herald*, on the other hand, relied on Bob Yeats, the paper's former chief sub-editor. He was actually in semi-retirement, and it is not unkind to recall that he was, in this new era of militancy and rapid change, completely out of his depth. In terms of energy and authoritative coverage of Scottish affairs, the *Glasgow Herald* in the 1970s was well behind both the *Scotsman* and the *Record*.

❛❜

One of the most remarkable aspects of Mackay's editorship was the extent to which he was a journalists' journalist. Andrew Hood, who served for a time as 'father' of the National Union of Journalists' chapel (local branch) on the *Scotsman*, tells of how, in the late 1960s, when Mackay was still deputy editor, he actually ordered Hood to hurry up and submit a substantial pay claim that would utilise the new concept of separate house agreements. During his editorship, Mackay was increasingly at war with the management of Thomson Regional Newspapers. For the most part, he kept his battles private, but the staff were aware that he was fighting for them.

Mackay was not an all-round editor, in that he was uneasy with what might be termed the more frivolous aspects of editorial innovation. When I was the paper's features editor in the late 1970s, I had difficulties with him over some of our more outlandish contributors. He was uneasy with Jack McLean, whom I had met when he was an official in the National Union of Students. I hired Jack to write a city diary. Jack deliberately wrote in a coarse way specifically designed to infuriate the Edinburgh bourgeoisie. But his copy was very, very funny.

Mackay was also uneasy with some of my stunts, such as when I splashed some doggerel poems by Alan Bold about Scotland's World Cup hopes in Argentina in 1978 all over the front of the weekend section. (Bold was, among many other talents, a brilliant book-reviewer and a fine poet, whom I used to complement the exceptional team of literary contributors, Robert Nye, Isobel Murray and Allan Massie.)

My biggest battle with Eric Mackay was to get him to sanction our proposed restaurant column. All major newspapers have food critics nowadays, but in the late 1970s the idea of regular restaurant reviews was regarded as light-minded and even degenerate. The proposed food critic was Conrad Wilson, who, as we have seen, was already writing fiery copy as a notably independent and controversial music critic. For those *Scotsman* readers who thought that the acme of musical bliss was an encore of Mozart's *Eine Kleine Nachtmusik* in the Usher Hall, Conrad had become public enemy number one.

When Mackay heard that I wanted Conrad, a dedicated gourmet who loved his food almost as much as his music, to bring his special blend of critical fastidiousness and constant combativeness to restaurant-reviewing, he said simply and firmly: No. But I persisted, and Conrad's 'Gut Reaction' column at last appeared. Needless to say, it was to prove the most controversial single feature in the entire paper. Although Mackay's successor, Chris Baur, precipitately ditched the column in 1985, it was for seven years a guaranteed spring of contention, fury and dispute. It was also, for the growing number of *Scotsman* readers who enjoyed spending money on eating out, a useful guide and a source of enlightenment.

These were battles I had with Mackay; but they were civilised. He was an equable and fair editor. I only once saw him seriously angry. That was in the summer of 1979. The paper sponsored a parachuting and skydiving team, based at Strathallan Airfield in Perthshire. One day, the *Scotsman's* marketing manager and the leader of the parachuting team came to me and proposed that the *Scotsman* should undertake a charity parachute jump for complete novices at Strathallan. I thought that this was a good idea – without really thinking it through.

The outing proved very popular: more than twenty journalists and marketing-department personnel turned up at Strathallan on a very windy Saturday morning. In retrospect, the event was a disaster waiting to happen. The conditions were not propitious; the wind was not only strong, but also swirling in various directions. Because so many had turned up, the 'training' was rushed. The plane that was to take us up to 2,800 feet for the jumps was tiny; there was only room for the pilot, the jumpmaster and three jumpers. It would have to make eight separate flights. We had all nurtured this vague idea of jumping out of the back of a big plane, as in the movies. The reality was nerve-wrackingly different. It transpired that, when the pilot cut the engine, we had to clamber out to the wing strut and then throw ourselves backwards. This was not likely to be a very happy experience for those, such as myself, who had a fear of heights.

Late in the afternoon, we were supposedly ready. The plane took off (piloted by the eminent QC and one-time appropriator of the Stone of Destiny, Ian Hamilton) and rapidly reached the required height. The engine cut; we all gazed up intently. The first jumper appeared, and the parachute billowed. So far, so good. But then it was apparent that something was far wrong. Our first parachutist was descending far from the little airfield. He disappeared behind some trees about a mile away. And this experience was repeated. Most of us – particularly the impractical journalists; the marketing executives proved much more adept at steering their descent with their parachute toggles, as instructed – found ourselves drifting well away from the airfield. I was lucky: I landed in a cornfield. My friend and colleague, Julie Davidson, who was shortly to become my wife, landed on a patch of hard-baked ground between two pigsties.

Three others were seriously unlucky. One landed on a barn roof, slid off and hit the roof of a side building, then slid off again to hit the ground in completely the wrong manner. He, and two others, sustained broken legs. The staff at the nearby Bridge of Earn hospital were not amused as first one, then another, then a third casualty were driven to their receiving unit. On the Sunday evening, Julie and I visited our three injured colleagues in the hospital. I realised then that I would face ructions on the Monday morning. One of our colleagues was going to be off work for a good six months, and the other two for about six weeks.

I arrived in the office expecting to be upbraided, but I was not prepared for the depth of Mackay's anger. He was furious on three counts. First, I had not told him about the foolhardy stunt. Second, the debacle had made the front page of that Monday's *Record*. Third, he was to lose three members of staff for some considerable time. He was almost speechless with fury – and, looking back, I can hardly blame him.

❛❜

Mackay presided over what Andrew Hood regards as the only real golden age that the paper enjoyed in the entire twentieth century. Hood reckons that this golden age ended almost overnight on 1 March 1979, when the Scottish people voted in favour of an Assembly but did not pass the 40 per cent test which had been made part of the Scotland Act – the legislation which set up the referendum – thanks to some assiduous parliamentary manoeuvring by a Labour backbencher called George Cunningham, an honourably recalcitrant Scot who represented a London constituency. The fact that the referendum produced an effective 'no' to devolution, although a majority of those who voted were in favour, was a devastating blow to both Mackay and his deputy Arnold Kemp – and indeed to the paper. The *Scotsman's* purpose and momentum were immediately lost. The staff sensed that Mackay, their leader and champion, was losing his way.

Internal bickering, hitherto virtually unknown, gathered pace with bewildering speed. The relations between Mackay and Kemp became fractious. They avoided public rows as far as they could, but we knew that matters were deteriorating at an alarming pace. Worse, many of the best journalists started to leave the paper. The exodus was undignified. I regret, in a way, that I was one of those who quit the *Scotsman* at that difficult time. Like several others, I should probably have shown more loyalty to a newspaper that had given me a wonderful decade, a decade in which journalism had seemed to be full of purpose and a genuine adventure. But loyalty is a rare commodity in journalism.

From the spring of 1979, the *Scotsman* haemorrhaged talent for a variety of reasons. The very first to leave was Neal Ascherson. Those who followed him included the paper's deputy Westminster editor, Tom James, the sportswriter Norman Mair, the feature-writer Julie Davidson, the precocious youngsters Sally Magnusson and Lionel Barber

(Lionel later became editor of the *Financial Times*), Angus Macleod, Jim Naughtie and of course Arnold Kemp, who at the beginning of 1981 left Edinburgh to edit the *Glasgow Herald*. The problem had been simply that the *Scotsman* had collectively assumed that the Assembly was going to happen, and that the paper would be at the very heart of the new Scotland. When it became clear that the Assembly was not going to materialise, the paper suddenly seemed hollow, a husk.

The lesson is that no newspaper should become too concerned with one particular campaign to the point of obsession. Fine if it wins; terrible if it loses. Cynics would say that newspapers should only embark on campaigns they know they are going to win; but that was too cynical a thought for the *Scotsman* in the 1970s. It was a glorious period on a great paper. The trouble was that we all thought we were going somewhere exciting; as it happened, we were just progressing blindly to oblivion. Or maybe that is too harsh; the devolution issue was not going to go away. What happened twenty years later, when Scotland regained her Parliament after almost 300 years, was to a large extent due to the softening-up process which the *Scotsman* had undertaken, almost single-handedly, in the 1960s and the 1970s. The *Scotsman* had blazed the trail.

Mackay stayed on for a few more years; he retired in 1985. Andrew Hood believes that his final years as editor were spent in debilitating guerrilla warfare with the Thomson Regional Newspapers management, trying to protect what was left of his paper's status as Scotland's national newspaper. He was a fine and distinguished editor, but the end of his editorship was an unfortunate coda to his great years.

Perhaps unfairly, I asked Andrew Hood to compare Dunnett and Mackay. He is in no doubt that Mackay was the better editor. 'Mackay was really editing the paper from the early 1960s onwards. Dunnett in effect dumped the whole burden on to him. Yet Mackay was nearly betrayed when it emerged that Alastair Stuart was Dunnett's preferred candidate as his successor. Dunnett's best years were early on. He was a romantic, a dreamer who could not be bothered with the nitty-gritty. The one dream that he did actually bother to develop was devolution.'

Hood sums up thus: 'Mackay was not very imaginative, he was often difficult to fathom, but he was a great editor. Through the years from the late 1960s to 1979, the *Scotsman* was in tune with Scottish public opinion. That is not to say that everyone agreed with the *Scotsman's* line; far from it. But, although not everyone agreed, it seemed that everyone was interested, and everyone responded. There was a huge uptake in the letters to the editor. For the first time, they became a central part of the paper.'

❛❜

One of the reasons why so many journalists left the *Scotsman* so quickly was because a new paper was being launched in the west. One of my pals on the *Scotsman* had been Ian Buchan, an exceptionally gifted sub-editor who had joined the *Scotsman* from the *Guardian* in 1971 and had immediately set about livening the place up. Ian was always well informed. Towards the end of the 1970s, Ian went through to Glasgow to work for his old pal Charles M. Wilson, who was then editing the *Evening Times*. Late in 1980, Ian phoned me to say he had heard that his boss was working on a top-secret project. He reckoned it was a new Sunday paper that was going to be launched by the Outram Group, owners of the *Evening Times* and the *Herald*.

At first, I did not believe Ian; the *Herald* had struggled though the 1970s, its journalism was tired and old-fashioned, it had just come through a long and debilitating industrial dispute and it had spent the incredible sum of £16 million in moving the very short distance eastwards across Glasgow from its Mitchell Street base to the old Express building in Albion Street. It was well known, in other words, that Outram's were now strapped for cash. Further, you did not need to be an economist to appreciate that times were hard. The new Thatcher government was grappling with the problems of an incipient recession; but, unlike most previous governments, it was refusing to spend more to ameliorate the growing problems. The climate for launching a paper could hardly have been worse. But the rumours became persistent – and then, early in 1981, I got a call from Charles Wilson, who wanted to meet me, urgently, in Glasgow.

I am not always the best reader of people, but it took me only about five seconds to work out that Charles was very different from the rather leisurely and mild-mannered people I had been working with in Edinburgh. I sensed immediately that here was a hard, dynamic, single-minded man whom you would cross at your peril. Charles came quickly to the point. He gave me the hardest of hard sells about his new paper, to be called the *Sunday Standard*. He told me I was lingering in a backwater and that the Outram Group was the future. I was in my early thirties, at a crucial point in my career. I'd be a fool not to move west and join the new project. If he had told me this a couple of years earlier, I'd have laughed out loud. And I'd have been both furious and scornful. But sadly, I did now think that the *Scotsman* was losing its way. The ebbs and flows in a newspaper's spirit and confidence are alarmingly swift.

Further, the money Charles was offering was considerably more than I was getting as features editor of the *Scotsman*. (This was a function not only of Charles's generosity but also of pay rates at the *Scotsman*. The paper's editorial staff had been disgracefully underpaid through the golden age, despite the best efforts of their editor. The anger and resentment at last spilled over in the form of a bitter strike in the spring of 1981, shortly after the *Sunday Standard* was launched in Glasgow.)

Charles wanted me to be features editor of his new paper, and gave me a week to make my decision. I had decided to say yes when we had our second meeting seven days later. Charles changed tack. He now asked me if I'd like to be his sports editor. (I later learned that he had decided on someone else as features editor.) He talked, forcefully and persuasively, about the need for fresh, innovative sports features. Scottish sportswriting was routine and parochial. He enthused me, though I should have been suspicious as to why I was no longer being offered the features job. I pointed out that I was not a production man. Surely the oversight of the production of the sports pages on Saturdays would be a key part of the sport editor's remit?

'Don't you worry', Charles said. 'I've just the man to handle all that. Your job will be to develop exciting new sports features and to handle a high-powered team of sportswriters.' Then, his clinching argument: 'You won't even need to work on Saturdays. Your work will be done during the week.' (Before long, I was starting work at 8am every Saturday morning, and I was lucky if I had finished work by midnight. But Charles was always the master of the brutally hard sell.)

I swithered for a few days before finally deciding to leave the *Scotsman*. Funnily, what clinched the decision was sheer sentiment. I am a Glaswegian – and, although my family had left the city when I was four, I was aware that Glasgow was *the* Newspaper City. It was the place where reputations were made – and where the bodies were buried. And, indeed, I'd say now that every Scottish journalist should try, if at all possible, to work for at least some of his or her career in Glasgow.

When I told him I wanted to go, Eric Mackay was remarkably considerate; he said he'd not hold me to my contract and would allow me to go almost immediately. And the *Scotsman* staff gave me a most generous farewell party. This was specially appreciated because so many people were leaving at the time. So, I still felt a little guilty and confused when I went to Glasgow and reported for duty for the first time at the famous Albion Street premises which had housed in turn the *Scottish Daily Express*, the *Scottish Daily News* and the *Glasgow Herald*. It was the most famous newspaper 'house' in Scotland, and these premises were to be my spiritual home for the next nineteen years. That Saturday afternoon and evening, we were producing the first of two dummy editions of the fledgling *Sunday Standard*.

I met some of those who were to become good colleagues, including Bob Jeffrey and Doug Gillon. Of the two leading sportswriters who had been hired, Ian 'Dan' Archer and Norman Mair, there was no sign. But then, this was a production run-through. So much for the way Charles had beguiled me into the job. A terrific, noisy, wisecracking crew of *Evening Times* sub-editors – men with an immense knowledge of football in particular and sport in general – went seriously enough through the motions of producing the paper. When all seemed complete, the newly hired sports staff adjourned downstairs to the Press Bar for a few pints. What I wrote above is wrong; it was the Press Bar that was to be my spiritual home. What a pub.

I did not witness too many examples of Charles's famous temper, though Doug Gillon recently reminded me that once, when I bravely but erroneously and stupidly told Charles that he was not fit to be an editor, his response was to stride across his office and bang his forehead against the wall. I did, however, once see an outburst of superbly mercurial, theatrical fury. It was as if the Third World War was breaking out. Charles was looking at the page plans, spread out neatly on a large table, for the sports features section. For some time, he said nothing, and the tension mounted palpably. His mouth was twitching, and he had turned pale. Eventually, in a storm of almost demonic anger, he rolled the plans into a huge bundle and marched off, clutching the bundle ahead of him as if it were noxious, in the direction of the toilets, followed by his sheepish sports team. Charles stuffed the plans down the first WC he came to, trampling them into the bowl and then furiously attempting to flush them away. There's only one f—ing place for this f—ing shite, he kept shouting.

It was my first experience of a scale-ten Charles Wilson tantrum. North Bridge it wasn't. Of course, most of the time, Charles was not like that at all. He had a fierce and very real temper, but he was always in control. He deployed his temper as a weapon; to some extent, he operated on fear. He was a shrewd man-manager. He knew that at least some journalists responded better to the 'more in sorrow than in anger' approach than to loud bollockings.

Charles had been brought up in the East End of Glasgow, in a household where the preferred paper was, significantly, the *Scottish Daily Express*. He had started his career as a copy boy on the *People* in London, and had worked on a vast variety of papers before returning to Glasgow in 1976 as editor of the *Evening Times*. During his national service with the Royal Marines, he had been a successful boxer. A small, lean, balding man, he was a life force.

His energy was extraordinary. He had launched the *Sunday Standard* in less than twenty weeks, from conception to first edition, which appeared on 26 April 1981. The excessive speed was predicated on fear that another house (probably the *Scotsman*) would launch a rival, or at least a spoiler. (The *Scotsman* had flirted with the notion of a Sunday paper in the bitter aftermath of the devolution referendum fiasco. Arnold Kemp had produced a few dummy editions, but there was no real commitment to the project.) There was also a rumour that Charles was worried that the Outram's management would take fright and back off, so he worked frantically to make the paper a reality before they had second thoughts.

Charles brought all his zest to the editing of the paper – almost too much so. Every day, he had been through all the papers – and I mean reading them, not skimming them – before he came into work. His sense of what was newsworthy – something that cannot really be taught – was instinctive and certain. His eagerness for immediacy and his boiling, broiling energy meant that he took some time to judge the *Sunday Standard*'s rhythm correctly. During the first few weeks, we were producing virtually a complete paper by Wednesday night, and then another by Friday. These two 'papers' were ripped up, and we started all over again, producing the actual paper that appeared on the Sunday in just two days. Slowly, Charles got the weekly pace right. He eased up and allowed the momentum to build gradually through the week. Tuesday became ideas day, an endless stimulating session in which all sorts of ideas and stunts were discussed and tossed around between departments. The real work started, slowly, on Wednesday. Saturdays were frenetic.

The paper had high editorial quality, but it was not flawless. Various crucial errors were made, though there was so much excitement in the early months that none of us really noticed them. Charles himself made a serious error in that he was too aggressively ambitious in his circulation target. He had trumpeted a circulation of 175,000; after the heady first few editions, the paper's sale settled at about 40,000 less. This was a very considerable achievement; yet, because of Charles's almost bombastic promise of a 175,000 sale, the highly creditable figure that was actually achieved was regarded by envious outsiders as a failure.

Secondly, although a very talented – and very well-paid – editorial team had been assembled, scant attention was directed towards the necessary back-up from distribution and advertising staff. Few, if any, extra personnel were hired in those areas; instead, the existing Outram's staff were expected to add the *Standard*'s requirements to their workloads, in return for not particularly generous bonuses, which contrasted with the largesse being given to the chosen journalists. This was absurdly unrealistic.

Thirdly, and very surprisingly, given Charles's well-earned reputation as a great newsman, the paper's carefully assembled investigations unit flopped. The three journalists hired – George Hume, David Scott and Roddy Forsyth – were in their different ways very able, and Hume and Scott were both widely experienced and highly respected. Roddy was much younger and very eager; he had edited the *Carnoustie Times* before returning to his native Glasgow to work on various papers including the *Herald*. Yet the unit produced few decent stories; perhaps the three journalists did not gel as a team. Roddy was soon hanging around the sports desk, offering to help out in any way he could. The lack of success of the unit reflects the continuing failure of the Scottish press to undertake serious investigative journalism in a consistent way. There are occasional spasms of impressive activity but no long-running and deep pursuit of the truth that is to be found in dark places.

The unit had every advantage: it was kept apart from the *Standard*'s main news operation, and it reported directly to Charles and his deputy Jack Crossley, not to the news editor. It was given money and time. It was under the direct management of one of the finest editors and news journalists of his generation. Yet it must be regarded as a failure. Significantly, Roddy and David and George all went on to resume their hitherto successful careers elsewhere.

And finally, the *Standard* was a sore source of division and even recrimination within the Albion Street building. (It did not help that the *Standard*'s editorial offices were high on the sixth floor, above the management offices and the executive suite; the *Evening Times* and *Glasgow Herald* journalists laboured far below on the second floor.) And Charles had made a point of hiring few people from the *Herald*. This was, he asserted, because he was determined not to dilute the paper in any way; but several *Herald* journalists chose to regard his tactic as a deliberate rejection by the man who had been, briefly, their editor. There was less of a problem with the *Evening Times*, because many of their production staff were helping to produce the *Standard* on Saturdays, and were well paid for doing so.

Furthermore, one or two of the *Standard* staff, who should have known better, flaunted their high salaries and their lavish expenses in the Press Bar at the bottom of the building – the Press Bar was always a volatile as well as a convivial watering hole – and this understandably antagonised some *Herald* staffers. In retrospect, it was clear that, if one paper was going to fail, it would be the new Sunday, not the old daily; but some of the editorial team of the *Standard* behaved as if their new paper was God's gift to Outram's, to Glasgow and indeed to Scotland.

The tyro editor of the *Glasgow Herald*, Arnold Kemp, tried manfully not to resent the high-spending paper four floors above, though its expensive, draining presence meant that he was starved of the resources he desperately needed to revive the *Herald*. He took to referring to the *Standard* as 'the greedy bairn upstairs', but he was, in public at any rate, supportive of the Sunday venture. And Arnold was a canny enough newspaperman to understand that, although the *Standard* journalists were paid much better than the *Herald* ones, there were not very many of them: the first editions of the *Standard* were produced by an editorial team of only thirty-four.

❜❜

Just over a year after the successful launch of the paper, Charles surprised us by announcing that he was soon departing to work for Rupert Murdoch in London, as number three on the *Times*. He rapidly went on to become deputy editor, and then editor, of that august paper – just in time to mastermind the move to Wapping, that great set piece in 1986 which proved to be a historic watershed in the modern history of the British press. The plan was to move the *Times* titles to Wapping in east London, where a new plant was set up with new computerised technology installed. This allowed the journalists to input their copy directly instead of going through the production unions. The production of newspapers had been subject to anarchy, not least because so many separate unions were involved in the process and could separately shut production down.

Of all Rupert Murdoch's editorial executives, Charles was most engaged in the secret planning of the move to Wapping. This involved the invention of a proposed paper, the *London Post*, which was allegedly to be produced at the new plant. That this elaborate subterfuge fooled so many people, including supposedly savvy journalists and print workers, is a tribute to Charles's political skills – and his cunning. Once the unions realised what was happening, there was sustained and frightening violence around the Wapping plant for almost a year. But the papers came out, and the victory was won. As with the miners' strike the previous year, there was a sense of unease. People sensed that the victory was both inevitable and necessary, but on the other hand there was huge disquiet about the manner in which the victory was actually achieved.

Charles had been so closely associated with the *Sunday Standard*, as both its founder and its inspirational leader, that it inevitably lost momentum after his departure. Jack Crossley took over, but the paper missed Charles's snap and bite. One or two of the staff started drifting away, including me: Arnold Kemp asked me to join him at the *Herald* as executive editor. I left the *Standard* in September 1982 after just eighteen months of fun-filled, happy journalism.

I had been privileged to work with two great sportswriters, Ian Archer and Norman Mair; but, looking back, I reckon that the best contributions to the pages were made by Doug Gillon, an all-rounder with the most encyclopaedic knowledge of sport of any journalist I have ever met. Doug's first love was, and remains, athletics, but he was a genuine expert on everything from boxing to volleyball. Charles's main requirement of the sports team was that we should produce a constant stream of unusual, provocative and innovative sports features – and we certainly did that.

By the spring of 1983, it was clear that the paper was losing its way, and the staff started preparing for the inevitable. The *Standard* had become an unacceptable drain on the resources of both the *Herald* and the *Evening Times*. It had been launched in a hurry, and the finances had never been propitious. Lonrho, the owners of Outram's, had not been particularly beneficent; the paper was financed out of borrowing and had to service the borrowing out of revenue. It ran up debts of over £5 million, and it had exemplified an old but sad truth: editorial excellence is no protection against financial reality. Although Arnold Kemp had been careful not to criticise the *Standard* in public, he was, I suspect, highly relieved when it closed in the summer of 1983. He had already invigorated the *Herald*, which had been pretty moribund during the 1970s. But the *Standard* was undoubtedly an incubus, diverting both resources and management focus.

The mechanics of the *Standard*'s closure were handled, with surprising finesse, by Terry Cassidy, the Herald Group's new managing director. He was an abrasive businessman from Teesside who had arrived at Albion Street early in 1982 from the *Irish Times* in Dublin, a paper whose fortunes he had turned around. I firmly believe that Cassidy is one of the unsung heroes of modern Scottish newspapers, if a most unlikely one. His first employment was as a professional footballer with Nottingham Forest. Then he had become involved in managing clubs (night, not football). Eventually, he drifted into the advertising side of newspapers in his home town, Middlesbrough. He had rapidly made his name as a tough, bruising commercial manager.

With the *Standard* now just a fond memory, Kemp and Cassidy could really concentrate on reviving the *Herald*. The paper had been through some bad years and was jaded. Arnold set about reinvigorating it, not so much by hiring new staff as by reigniting the spark in the many talented writers and sub-editors on the existing payroll. He made people believe in themselves again. This was particularly true of the writing staff. I don't think it is patronising to note that Arnold breathed new life into the careers of many fine journalists.

Editors, like generals, require luck, and Arnold had one huge stroke of luck. He was appointed exactly two years before the *Herald's* bicentenary was to be celebrated. Celebrated is perhaps the wrong word, because one or two of the paper's staffers told me later that they had been dreading the anniversary; they felt their paper was going nowhere, and that the bicentenary would be an embarrassment. Arnold quickly realised that the bicentenary in fact offered him a public-relations godsend. He used it to make clear that the venerable paper was embarking on its third century with a renewed sense of zest and purpose.

The journalist Murray Ritchie recalls that the *Herald* had been a grim place in the late 1970s. 'Although the circulation was going up, that was just because the *Herald* picked up some of the *Scottish Daily Express* sales, almost without trying, after its demise. It was a pretty hellish time. What Arnold did was to raise not just the circulation figures, but the quality of the paper also. That was some achievement. He picked out various people on the staff and went out of his way to encourage them, and he made sure that the paper was always full of interest and controversy. He gave it courage, he took risks and he got it talked about. The *Glasgow Herald* had been hopelessly right-wing and anti-devolution. That had been changing before Arnold arrived, but he made the paper champion the devolution cause in a way that would have been unthinkable ten years earlier.'

One of those whose careers Arnold revived was Ian Bruce, one of the harder reporters, a great union man, who had become disillusioned. He recalls: 'The *Herald* was dying in the late 1970s. Arnold arrived and created an anti-authority culture in what had been an establishment paper. He was a rebel. He gave us a freedom of action that we hadn't enjoyed before, and he supported us.' Ian Bruce repaid Arnold personally during the Falklands War in 1982, a conflict that he covered superbly. He was the sole reporter from a Scottish paper with the task force. He survived being bombed and strafed by Argentinian planes at Ajax Bay, he witnessed the blowing-up of HMS *Antelope*, and he was one of only two journalists to accompany 45 Commando on their hazardous and arduous 'yomp' over to Port Stanley. He says: 'About 35 per cent of the forces were Jocks, and they did most of the fighting. It was vital to have a Scottish reporter with them. I'd trained with the Paras on the ship all the way down, and I was ready for it.' Bruce's exceptionally graphic dispatches were published by every Scottish daily paper and were regularly quoted on radio and television. This was the biggest rolling story there had been for several years, with Bruce – and therefore the *Herald* – at the very heart of it.

❛❜

Arnold Kemp enjoyed making mischief, and he was flamboyant. On the *Scotsman*, he had been, if not exactly erratic, certainly given to working in fits and starts. Now, he worked long hours with a concentrated intensity. At the same time, he was always lively, always open-minded and not averse to a little judicious attention-seeking. This was reflected in the paper: where it had been staid and dull, it was now cheeky and challenging.

Put like that, the process sounds easy, almost straightforward; but it wasn't. Turning round the *Glasgow Herald*, which had been moribund, required an editor with self-belief, purpose and confidence, one who felt that his career had led inexorably to this moment. Arnold had become editor at exactly the right time, for both himself and the paper. When he took up the great *Scotsman* theme of devolution, he well realised that it would not be such a fashionable cause in the 1980s, though he had staunch allies in senior Labour politicians such as Donald Dewar, who later told me that he regarded the *Herald* with 'exasperated affection'.

Boldly, Arnold tilted the paper sharply to the left. Its Unionism had become tired and intellectually slack. This was the very period when the British right was being energised by Thatcherism, which Arnold had no time for. He took on the paper's natural constituency – the business and mercantile classes of Glasgow – but in a respectful, non-confrontational way. Even so, there was, for a time, genuine concern in the West of Scotland business community, and there was talk in boardrooms, golf clubs and cocktail bars of advertising boycotts or even attempted takeovers.

Luckily, this kind of nonsense annoyed Terry Cassidy even more than it annoyed Arnold, particularly when it transpired that some business leaders had bypassed Cassidy and had directly approached the Lonrho headquarters in the City of London. (Geoffrey Parkhouse, the political editor, who was always zealous in maintaining good Lonrho contacts, tipped off Terry and Arnold about this.) Terry Cassidy was actually a much better businessman than most of the dinosaurs who were ineptly plotting against the *Herald*. Although he and Arnold had the occasional spectacular row, their relationship was essentially one of mutual respect and support. Anyway, Lonrho's executives treated the mutterings in Glasgow with the contempt they deserved. Cassidy was providing them with big profits, and that was all they wanted.

Funnily enough, some of the senior writers on the paper, people like the wine correspondent and leader-writer Bob McLaughlan, John Weyers the letters editor, and Ronnie Dundas the business editor, and (to a much lesser extent) Geoffrey Parkhouse himself, were men of the right. Arnold kept them onside with his charm and the freedom he gave them; indeed, they flourished under his editorship. And they were not mugs; they well understood that the paper had been reborn and that the circulation was rising fast.

The *Herald*'s journey leftwards under Arnold signalled that it had indeed changed and was in tune with the times – for, in Scotland, Thatcherism was detested and the Tories were in freefall. But the stance of the paper was never easy to define: critics would often aver that politically it lacked focus and was confused. This was because Arnold was far more interested in ideas and good writing than in rigorous consistency.

Bob McLaughlan and I drew the line when the paper actually flirted with unilateral nuclear disarmament – for a time the official policy of the Labour opposition at Westminster – because we believed very strongly that the Cold War still had to be won. Arnold, I am pleased to recall, was persuaded that unilateralism would have been a journey too far for a paper that had traditionally shared with the *Scottish Daily Express* the role of flagship of the right. But of course the *SDE* had collapsed in 1974, brought down by militants, and the *Herald* had now moved to the left, so it was perhaps little wonder that some of those on the right in Scotland were angry because they no longer had a paper speaking up for them.

But I reckon that Arnold's ultimate strength as an editor was that, although a fascinated and occasionally despairing student of politics, he was never on any kind of sustained party-political mission. Nor was he all that interested in news. He had never been a reporter, and he once confessed to me that the worthy 'paper of record' stories on the daily news schedule often bored him. What he wanted was flair and mischief and, above all, fine, though not fancy, writing. He encouraged his executives, whose specific duties did not necessarily involve writing, to write as much as they wanted. This worked wonderfully with Ann Donaldson, the paper's London editor; perhaps less so with the paper's features editor, Ray Gardner, who was possibly over-indulged.

During his golden decade, between 1981 and 1991, Arnold hired surprisingly few journalists from other papers. A notable quartet arrived from the *Scotsman* – Jack McLean, Julie Davidson, Andrew Hood and Alf Young – and a few well-chosen youngsters came from local papers. He also found an executive job for Jack Webster, who had been operating as a freelance. Arnold's criteria when hiring were unusual, if refreshing. When the paper's music critic, Malcolm Rayment, retired, Arnold pondered long before hiring as his successor Michael Tumelty, who was a teacher with scant journalistic background. When asked why Tumelty, he replied simply that, of all the candidates, Tumelty was the one who wrote best.

Arnold was consistently and refreshingly open to ideas. In 1984, Jack Webster wrote for the *Herald* an insightful and sensitive profile of Robin Jenkins, then generally regarded as Scotland's pre-eminent living novelist. Jack revealed that Jenkins had taken to writing novels that he then couldn't be bothered to send to publishers. (His relations with his various publishers – nine of them altogether – were often difficult.) The typescripts lay, literally, in a bottom drawer in his house at Toward, above his beloved Clyde estuary.

Jack's revelation prompted a minor outcry. There was indignation in Scotland's literary community and beyond. Why was this exceptional Scottish novelist writing just for himself, rather than a wider public? Somewhat presumptuously, I decided that the *Herald* should play its part in bringing at least one of these unpublished novels to the light of day. This was where Arnold showed his mettle. He took up the idea enthusiastically, and supported Jack and me as we persuaded first the novelist himself and then a publisher to go ahead with the project. The good offices of the paper, and the authority of the editor, were absolutely crucial. The novel chosen was *The Awakening of George Darroch*, an important historical and religious novel about the Great Disruption of 1843.

The point here is that Arnold was prepared to take a risk in an area where newspapers do not normally get involved. And he was open-minded. Too many editors are only interested in their own ideas. This is especially problematic if they never have ideas – and, strange as it may seem, some of the duller editors don't. But the better editors have this gift of backing other people's ideas with enthusiasm and commitment.

❝ ❞

Arnold knew of my long friendship with Jack McLean and told me that he wanted Jack to go places where people did not expect him to be. If this had been taken literally, it would have meant anywhere but a pub. Jack was not yet a full-time journalist – he was still teaching on Glasgow's south side – but I came up with a few stunts. Through the good offices of Mike Haggerty, the *Herald's* rowing correspondent, we got Jack a VIP 'access all areas' accreditation to the Oxford and Cambridge boat race in London, where he hobnobbed with the likes of Denis Thatcher. Jack wrote about this anachronistic occasion with a wonderful satirical edge. But what made his copy outstanding was that he was not cruel; there was affection in what he wrote as well. Then, through a contact in the Scottish Police Federation, I managed to get Jack invited to that body's annual residential meeting at Peebles Hydro. Again, the copy was superb. Jack reckoned it was the only gathering at which he had ever been systematically outdrunk.

This was essentially frivolous; but the emphasis on the quality of writing was anything but frivolous. It was particularly brave in the 1980s, a decade when the nature of journalism was changing; it was becoming more hard-edged, more tightly subbed, possibly reflecting the harsher aspects of Thatcherism.

In 1988, I was approached by Thomson Regional Newspapers to see if I was prepared to be the editor of the newly launched *Scotland on Sunday*. After various discussions, I was seriously tempted. Arnold played the situation brilliantly. On the one hand, he encouraged me to go, saying he did not want to stand in my way; on the other, he told me he'd be overjoyed if I stayed. I decided to stay. Like the *Scotsman* in the 1970s, in the 1980s the *Herald* enjoyed a golden era.

In 1991, Arnold threw a huge party at Au Petit Riche, a venerable *fin-de-siècle* restaurant in Paris, to mark the tenth anniversary of his editorship. It was a grand, expansive gesture – Arnold took over the entire restaurant – and the last of many in his editorship, though that was to last another three years. His senior journalists and most of the paper's senior management were present, as well as the *Herald's* wayward but fitfully brilliant Paris stringer, Nick Powell, his wife Véronique, and a few other French friends. We had arrived in Paris by different routes and different forms of transport, and the party somehow, despite the louche foreign locus, took on the aspect of a warm homecoming. Possibly the only flaw in an otherwise perfect night came when I had to make a speech in French.

Notably absent from this happy and stylish occasion was Liam Kane. This was not a snub; Liam had only just arrived at the *Herald*, after the invitations had been issued and the arrangements made. Liam was marketing director; within a few months, he had become managing director of Outram's, and within a year he had concluded the management buy-out that ended Lonrho's ownership and turned Outram's into Caledonian Newspapers. Liam was a man in a hurry – too much of a hurry for Arnold, who was becoming a little tired. I chart the deteriorating relations between Arnold and Liam in Chapter 3; the point to note here is that Arnold should probably have retired on that tenth anniversary. He was only 52, and he still had much to do other than edit a newspaper. Like Dunnett and Mackay at the *Scotsman*, he had probably stayed on too long. The 1980s had been a wonderful, magical decade for him. That could not be said of the 1990s.

❝❞

George McKechnie, the last of the quintet of editors for whom I worked, took over at the *Herald* right at the end of 1994, after many years editing the *Evening Times*. George was a paradox. Superficially grumpy and dour, he was actually kind and considerate, and almost pastoral in his concern for his journalists. A very large man, he had more physical presence, and menace, than any of the other editors I have described, even Charles Wilson. When George left his office to walk the floor, people were instantly aware that the boss was on the prowl, and there was a palpable frisson of tension.

He was a workaholic: he was the first journalist in the office every morning, at 7:30 before the cleaners had departed, and he was often not away until after 9pm. I suspect that he rather resented it on the few occasions when I was in before him or worked later than he did. News was his staple, and at first his editorial conferences were long – interminably so – as he went through every news story on the schedule in excruciating detail, asking question after question of the embattled news editor, Colin McDiarmid, and making not a few suggestions (well, commands) into the bargain. The word on the editorial floor was that Colin was fighting for his job; but I don't think this was the case. George had identified, before he took over, the five senior journalists he wanted to ease out, and Colin wasn't one of them. What was going on was rather different: Colin, and the rest of us, were effectively being told that the tide had turned. News, once again, was king. George and Colin were soon working very well together.

George told me that he needed me to provide continuity and to explain to him the more recondite aspects of the *Herald*'s undoubtedly complex chemistry. He also told me to come up with some more features stunts. The best of these was when we asked Jill Crawshaw, an award-winning travel journalist from London, to tour Scotland at the back end of the tourist season as a lone but curious and enthusiastic female traveller with money to spend – but to some extent acting the daft lassie. The incompetence, indifference and sheer grubbiness that she encountered across the length and breadth of Scotland's so-called hospitality industry were appalling, and she wrote her experiences up in graphic detail, frankly but fairly. The results constituted an absolutely devastating series. It prompted a huge debate that went on for months, as well as a national conference that was convened in Glasgow. Heads rolled at the Scottish Tourist Board (as it then was), although, in fairness, the board was hardly responsible for much of the nonsense that Jill encountered. George was so delighted with this series that he told me he thought it was the making of his editorship.

This editorship lasted barely two years, but they were among the more effective and solid two years in the *Herald*'s long history. George was uneasy when his buddy Liam Kane departed after the takeover by Scottish Television in October 1996. George was, for reasons I could never quite fathom, suspicious of the motives of the two key men in the new ownership, Gus (later Lord) Macdonald and Andrew Flanagan. He certainly did not like their somewhat pernickety but relentlessly focused inquiring into all aspects of the paper's management.

George stood down at the start of 1997. He had succeeded Arnold Kemp, the man who was probably the most brilliant – with the possible exception of Sir William Robieson – editor of the *Herald* in the twentieth century. That was an almost impossible task, but one that he had accomplished with both dignity and efficiency.

❛❜

These, then, were the five editors I worked for. They were so different; one of the conclusions of this chapter is that it is almost impossible to define what makes a good editor. Much depends on the circumstances of the paper, relations with the proprietor and the mood of the times. But then, a good editor can change the circumstances of his paper, and a great editor can help to change the mood of the times. Like so much in our feverish, transitory world, the nature of the job is changing fast. These days, an editor has to be willing to spend more and more time with the likes of lawyers – our increasingly litigious society has had a huge impact on newspapers – and marketing executives. There is not so much that is romantic or exciting about newspapers these days; they are products. The magic and the mystery have all but gone.

If I had to categorise, in one word, what best encapsulated the editing essence of each of these men, each in his own way exceptional, I would write: Dunnett – showmanship; Mackay – purpose; Wilson – energy; Kemp – flair; McKechnie – solidity. As I have tried to show, I believe that Dunnett, Mackay and Kemp all stayed on too long; their editorships manifestly did not end anything like as well as they began.

It is, as they say, better to go out the front door with people clapping than out the back door with people shaking their heads. Or, as Harold Wilson put it when he retired as prime minister unexpectedly in 1976, it's much better to have them asking why you're going than asking why on earth you're staying. Who exactly are the 'them' in the context of newspapers? The staff? The readers? The management? The wider Scottish public? Probably a mixture of all four. Editors have so many constituencies to satisfy. The job is well nigh impossible. But I still reckon that to have the chance to edit a daily newspaper is to have a privilege almost beyond describing.

I am conscious that the five men I have described all had, to use a cliché, ink in their blood. They were all newspaper obsessives. This does not mean that they were anoraks or geeks. Far from it. But newspapers were as necessary to them as water is to a fish. Observing them, and working for them, I was aware that this was a quality I lacked. I love newspapers, and I had wanted to be a journalist since I was about ten. On the other hand, I could live without them; I did not have this overweening, almost physical need for newspapers to play a constant, key role in my life. In that sense, I was always a wee bit detached. I hope I was never a dilettante; but I could never quite enter that night-and-day, utterly obsessive world where the newspaper was, quite simply, the be-all and end-all of existence.

Alastair Dunnett, Eric Mackay, Charles Wilson, Arnold Kemp and George McKechnie were all special men and special editors. To work for them was far more than mere employment. It was both an education and a journey on an especially thrilling roller-coaster.

2

Further Thoughts on Editing

I have described, as scrupulously as I can, the styles and personalities of the five editors I worked for. I noted that three of them probably stayed *in situ* for too long. Since the 1990s, the turnover of editors has become much more rapid. If you had worked on the *Scotsman* between 1994 and 1999, you would have served under seven editors. This is obviously absurd. But the generally shorter span of Scottish editorships to some extent reflects the nature of their task – always difficult and now becoming nearly impossible.

Here are the views of three leading and very experienced journalists on editorship. Anne Simpson arrived at the *Glasgow Herald* in 1975 from the *Yorkshire Post*. In her distinguished thirty-plus years on the *Herald*, she has observed eight different editors at work. She says: 'The role of an editor is a bit like a referee: he's got to keep all the elements of his paper in balance at the same time as judging the best lead story for that night's edition. The best editors are the ones that can combine a serious commitment to disseminating information with an element of entertainment. And the distinction of the Scottish press is that it must inform the country about the issues for Scotland, and that's very important in countries that are small like Scotland and Ireland. A good press is a way of small countries having a voice against the big battalions in the world today, and I think that's very important. The Scottish press has to safeguard the issues that concern its readership. It's different from the British press as a whole, because, as we know, it's a different country with different values.'

Bob Jeffrey, who has worked on many roles on five different Glasgow papers, says: 'Part of it is stimulating your staff, controlling them, leading by example ... newspapers thrive on conferences, and the editor has to be a very, very good conference-controller. At the conference, you bring together the various department heads, who tell the editor their notions of what should be in the paper that night – but the editor decides, not them. Getting the paper out right on the night is difficult when you've thousands upon thousands of words in it. It's impossible for the editor to read every word, but an editor has got to be in total control. He's also got have a pretty good idea of what will sell his paper, what his readers are looking for. He's really got to be a polymath.'

And John McGurk, who has edited all three Edinburgh-based papers, the *Evening News*, *Scotland on Sunday* and the *Scotsman*, says: 'The modern editor has to be all things to all men. You've got to be a bit of a social worker, a PR person, a personnel man; you've got to be someone with a very strong commercial instinct. You've got to have marketing ability, to know how to promote your newspaper. And that's all on top of the basic job of editing, of selecting what goes where, and deciding what kind of balance there's going to be in the paper ... You have to produce a very interesting paper that has broad appeal but also maintains its substance and its depth.'

The editor of a pan-Scotland quality, such as the *Herald*, the *Scotsman*, the *Sunday Herald* or *Scotland on Sunday*, has to provide coverage at various different, and competing, levels. The paper should cover all important Scottish stories – and many of these stories are being covered in depth by Scotland's excellent local press – and then cover UK stories with authority also. This is expensive; the London staffs of the *Scotsman* and the *Herald* have diminished drastically since the mid-1980s, as management have increasingly regarded separate London offices as a luxury.

And finally, without being too pretentious, these papers have to cover the whole world – but they do not have access to a cadre of foreign correspondents. They have access to the various worldwide news agencies, and they can take syndicated material from other news groups, but by definition these sources do not provide exclusivity. The editor has little influence on the content of this copy. Scottish editors have improvised and finagled to make use of some excellent foreign stringers – that is, good local correspondents who are retained, but are not staff correspondents in the likes of Washington or Paris or Rome.

Ideally, a paper like the *Scotsman* or the *Herald* is attempting to provide everything – local, national, global – that a reasonably sophisticated and demanding reader would require, but on a relatively tiny budget. This task has always been hard enough; it was rendered infinitely more difficult in the early 1990s, a time of price wars in England, when the London houses suddenly discovered that Scotland was a soft circulation area, ripe for exploitation. So, they swamped Scotland with so-called Scottish editions. They hired a few Scottish journalists and claimed to be producing genuine Scottish papers. The key to their success was that they had access to huge marketing and promotion budgets – and, perhaps more significantly, they could project the copy of their famous byline staff journalists and columnists working in London and abroad. And, with their bigger specialist staffs, they could offer more sophisticated and detailed coverage of, for example, what was happening in the City.

Elsewhere in this book, Jack Webster notes that at least part of the phenomenal success of the *Scottish Daily Express* was based on its ability to use the world-famous giants whom Beaverbrook had cultivated carefully: writers such as Chapman Pincher and Sefton Delmer. But the paper remained quintessentially Scottish. With the best will in the world, no-one could argue that today's *Scottish Daily Mail*, for example, is quintessentially Scottish. Not surprisingly, the circulations of the *Herald* and the *Scotsman* have declined under this extreme pressure from London-based titles, though perhaps not by as much as might have been expected.

❛❜

Over the years, the Scottish dimension has given Scottish editors and editorial executives the opportunity to show what they were made of when they were being patronised by the London government or condescended to by the English establishment. Eric Mackay made his name as London editor of the *Scotsman* when he stood up to Lord Home, the then Commonwealth Secretary, who was seeking to censor the paper's forthright coverage of political unrest in Nyasaland (now Malawi) based on information provided by Church of Scotland missionaries in the field. The *Scotsman* was the only paper in the UK carrying detailed reports of brutalities being perpetrated by the government of Dr Hastings Banda, and Home summoned Mackay to his office in Whitehall. The minister demanded that he should both reveal his sources and cease to report what was going on in the country. Mackay walked out.

Much later, when Magnus Linklater was editing the *Scotsman* and Arnold Kemp was his counterpart at the *Herald*, the two men collaborated notably to scupper a piece of egregious impertinence from the Foreign Office. Murray Ritchie, then the *Herald*'s man in Brussels – the paper's only full-time foreign correspondent, a posting Arnold Kemp had fought long and hard for – found he was being excluded from the press lunches that were regularly held at the residence of the British Ambassador to the European Union. These lunches were used to provide Foreign Office background briefings, and Ritchie noted that his exclusion meant that he could not operate on equal terms with the rest of the British press corps. His treatment was giving the London papers an unfair advantage over their Scottish rival. When he complained, he was ludicrously informed by a Foreign Office official that the ambassador didn't like too many people at his table; he might have to raise his voice.

When Ritchie persisted, he was told that the real reason was that the *Herald* did not circulate in London (not true, though the paper's sales in London were admittedly meagre). At this time, Magnus Linklater appointed Chris McLaughlin as his European editor to work in Brussels. McLaughlin quickly joined forces with Ritchie. As the representations, now from two national papers, continued, the FO at last came up with a formal threefold response. This was that the ambassador's briefings were by tradition London-centric (possibly true), that UK ministers did not read Scottish papers (manifestly not true) and that, if Scots really wanted to find out what was going on in Europe, they could buy English papers (sheer insolence).

Magnus and Arnold took swift and concerted action. They warned the FO that, unless their European editors were given immediate access to the lunches, comprehensive accounts of the imbroglio would be published on the same day on the front pages of both papers. Murray Ritchie recalls that there was an instant response. He and Chris McLaughlin were taken to an expensive lunch by Foreign Office officials, and from then on there was no problem about their attending the ambassador's briefings. Murray claims that he has dined out on the tale of this shoddy but revealing episode ever since, well aware that its repetition infuriates the Foreign Office.

Magnus Linklater recalls: 'The attitude in Brussels was incredibly condescending to the Scottish press. It was really going back to the Victorian era: You will accept the news that we decide that you can have. And we were being edged out, we were being prevented from doing our job of actually reporting for a Scottish readership. And so we challenged that, and I'm delighted to say that we won. Between the two of us, between the *Herald* and the *Scotsman*, we managed to put Scotland on the map in Brussels.'

❛ ❜

The euphoria that greeted the election of New Labour in 1997 obscured the fact that a new and very tough and very sophisticated era of media control was upon us. New Labour had a huge majority, the prime minister Tony Blair was immensely popular, and the opposition was in a condition of fragmented ruin. Not surprisingly, this led to a certain hubris and arrogance in the government's dealings with the press, and it was a difficult time for editors. This was especially the case in Scotland, where at least some meaningful opposition was provided by the Scottish National Party in the twenty months between the referendum confirming devolution in the autumn of 1997 and the elections for the new Scottish Parliament in 1999.

I was editing the *Herald* then, and at first I was not particularly affected by this change in the media climate. I had for long enjoyed good relations with Donald Dewar, the politician who was clearly going to be First Minister in the new constitutional dispensation. Donald was a very bookish man; and, in a previous life as the *Herald*'s literary editor, I had regularly sent him books for review (and some not for review). He was, for such a thin, ascetic, intellectual man, a voracious eater – and, when I occasionally entertained him to a snack lunch in my office, I made sure that there was food for three or four people, even if Donald and I were unaccompanied.

I also enjoyed reasonable relations with Donald's press officer, David Whitton, a man whom I respected. So, it was a surprise when some of the more thuggish background figures around Donald started to campaign against the *Herald* in the spring of 1999, in the weeks leading up to the first elections for the new Parliament. It was being put about that the *Herald* was a nationalist paper, and that we were 'not worthy' – whatever that meant. One of Donald's aides actually phoned me up and demanded belligerently to know who had written a particular (perfectly reasonable) leader in the *Herald*. When I refused to tell him, I was told: 'Well, Harry, just you tell whoever wrote it that he must have a thistle jammed up his arse'. Needless to say, I also refused to comply with this 'command'.

We were certainly not a nationalist paper; our sin was to take the SNP seriously, and to report them fairly and comprehensively, unlike – alas – several other Scottish papers. But I felt that there was a bullying aspect to New Labour, who thought they were the only game in town at that time. The party had been in opposition for eighteen years, had reinvented itself and had smashed the Tories out of sight. It was on a wave. It felt that other political parties could be treated with arrogant contempt, and by extension the media could be treated with equal contempt. The papers could certainly be manipulated.

I only became aware that matters were becoming quite dangerous when it was very publicly revealed by one of Donald's backroom staff that a large amount of political advertising was being given to both the *Record* and the *Scotsman*. The advertising was worth more than £100,000 to each paper. It was also made clear that the *Herald* was not to receive any of this political advertising because we were 'not worthy' – that weasel phrase again. At this time, we were the only indigenous Scottish paper whose circulation was going up. That, and our perceived sympathy for the SNP, seemed to infuriate New Labour; one of the paradoxes of devolution, which they delivered effectively, was that they were becoming more and more London-centric.

Needless to say, the then owners of the *Herald*, the Scottish Media Group (Scottish Television, as was), were curious, to put it mildly, as to why we were not getting some very acceptable advertising revenue. But I am pleased to record that they never put me under any editorial pressure, though I'm sure that this was the ultimate point of this squalid little manoeuvre. In the event, the *Herald* never did receive its fair share of Labour's political advertising; but neither did our editorial policy or coverage deviate in any manner whatsoever. Donald Dewar stayed aloof during this episode; he distanced himself from it. In that sense, he was like Tony Blair: he kept well away from some of the dubious tactics of his henchmen. I wrote the *Herald's* eve-of-poll leader in May 1999. We offered no endorsement of any party, and instead called for a new Parliament which would make a real difference to Scotland, with a new style of politics. We had been fair to all the parties.

In a bizarre coda to the political-advertising episode, the *Herald* had another problem later in 1999. I had decided to launch the Scottish Politician of the Year Awards in order to encourage interest in, and high standards at, the new Parliament. SMG were keen backers of this project; but, even so, we needed generous sponsors, and the Scottish business community seemed singularly uninterested in supporting us. Eventually, through the good offices of my friend Michael Shea, the former press secretary to the Queen, a deal was brokered with Zurich Financial Services, a large financial conglomerate whose chief executive in London, Sandy (now Lord) Leitch, was a Fifer who took a keen interest in Scottish affairs. The first awards dinner, in the autumn of 1999, was a glittering occasion held in the main atrium of the Royal Scottish Museum. The recipient of the first Politician of the Year Award was to be none other than Donald Dewar – the obvious choice. But, forty-eight hours before the event, I was told, to my amazement, that no Labour MSPs would be attending the event. There was confusion both as to the reason for the boycott and as to who had organised it. Then, just twenty-four hours before it was to take place, I was told that there had been a rethink.

Donald Dewar did not have a particularly high regard for the Scottish press, but he once confided to me, during a discursive lunch at an Italian restaurant in the west end of Glasgow, that he would have liked to edit the *Herald*. As a loyal Glaswegian, he always retained his affection for the paper, and from time to time he wrote for it, always with cerebral force. He was an unlucky politician who had briefly flourished as a junior minister under Harold Wilson in the 1960s. Then he lost his seat. He won the Garscadden by-election in Glasgow in 1978; but, the next year, Mrs Thatcher won the general election, and he found himself in opposition – and he was to remain out of office for eighteen years. He once told me that he felt that many Old Labour MPs found opposition their natural condition, but he loathed it. One thing he did in those barren years was to work tirelessly to keep the cause of devolution alive when it had become unpopular and discredited in the Labour Party. And, of course, he was rewarded for his resilience and his consistency when he became, in the evening of his career, the 'Father of the Nation' who delivered devolution and was First Minister in the new Parliament.

I was chairman of the Scottish Editors Committee when Donald hosted a most pleasant dinner for us at his official residence, Bute House, in September 2000. He had been ill a month or so earlier, but I had never seen him in such sparkling form. He was full of happy nostalgia about his childhood holidays in Aberdeenshire. And, although he was in no way smug, he seemed, for the only time that I can recall, to be reflecting that his political career had been worthwhile. A month later, he opened the new *Herald* offices in Renfield Street, Glasgow. It was the last time I saw him alive – for, two days later, on Wednesday 11 October, he died. He was a fine Scot and a fine politician, dogged and decent, and I am sorry to note that his stock seems to have diminished rapidly since his death.

Many Scottish journalists, including myself, held him in the highest esteem. Deep down, he always understood that, in Enoch Powell's phrase, a politician who complains about the press is like a fish complaining about the sea. Scotland's pre-eminent living historian, Prof. Tom Devine, has judiciously noted that no measured judgment on Donald Dewar's overall career will be possible for quite some time. Many of us who fought and argued in our various ways for devolution are so far somewhat disappointed with the outcome. But I don't think that diminishes Dewar's achievement.

❝ ❞

The delivery of devolution was expected, among many other things, to be to the benefit of the indigenous Scottish press; this had been clearly understood by the two Scottish editors who had got the campaign for conditional change under way all those years previously, Alastair Dunnett and his successor at the *Scotsman*, Eric Mackay. If anything, devolution has had the opposite effect. Colin McClatchie, Rupert Murdoch's senior manager in Scotland, says: 'There was this expectation for the indigenous Scottish publishers that they would do better from the onset of devolution in sales terms than their national English counterparts selling in Scotland. The irony is that, in post-devolution Scotland, exactly the opposite has taken place, and the indigenous players have performed worse. So, for example, the *Times* is selling more copies in Scotland post-devolution than it was pre-devolution.' In part, this may be because, with the exception of the *Herald*, the indigenous Scottish papers have tended to be very critical of the new Parliament – its members, its proceedings, and of course its building.

Magnus Linklater, who ceased to be the *Scotsman* editor in 1994, comments on his former paper's performance when the new Parliament came into being five years later: 'At the time of devolution, it suddenly began questioning the whole venture, and it began to be highly critical of, and indeed hostile to, the whole enterprise. I felt at the time that that was out of synch with its own tradition. That's not to say that the *Scotsman* shouldn't have been very critical of some of the things that were going on. But it seemed to be almost viscerally opposed to the enterprise. I felt that was out of tune with its own tradition and to an extent out of tune with its own readers, and therefore a mistake.'

George Rosie, the senior Scottish journalist and commentator, who has a particular interest in architecture, says: 'The Scottish press still has to come to terms with our new Parliament. It is over-interested in trying to haul it down. I appreciate that newspapers have a duty to be critical, but I find an almost universal hostility. The Parliament building itself has done untold damage. It has created an atmosphere of constant querulousness. The saga of the building is one spectacular extended cock-up. The Scottish press picked that up and kept it going.'

Alan Cochrane, the Scottish political commentator for the *Daily Telegraph*, is by no means sympathetic to the new Parliament, yet he is surprisingly sympathetic to the indigenous Scottish press: 'The papers that are doing well are not indigenous and not part of the fabric of Scotland. And papers like the *Herald*, the *Scotsman* and the *Record* have suffered in the last year or so. I wonder if it's because they're not appreciated enough as national newspapers, as national institutions, as Scottish icons.'

Be that as it may, the current situation was certainly not foreseen by Alastair Dunnett and Eric Mackay, who virtually invented and then developed the notion of devolution and imposed it on the political classes. And it was most certainly never part of their game plan that the *Scotsman* itself should suffer with the arrival of devolution. Eric Mackay took the circulation of the *Scotsman* up to almost 100,000; at the time of writing (May 2006), it was 56,000, and the editor of the *Scotsman* since 2004, John McGurk, had just resigned.

It could be argued that, now that they have gained devolution, Scots are more confident and secure about their place and role within the UK, and therefore feel less need to assert their Scottishness through buying indigenous Scottish newspapers.

A different perspective comes from Magnus Magnusson, a veteran of the *Scottish Daily Express* and the *Scotsman*, and perhaps the best-known Scottish journalist of the past fifty years. He says: 'I believe that, when we get independence, a lot of it will be due to the way in which the Scottish press has not let the idea slip out of the public mind. That is, the constant reminders of what devolution is about, what the national identity is about, what independence is about. In twenty years' time, I expect to see an independent Scottish nation. Much of the credit for that will go to the Scottish press.'

3

Much Ado about Megalomaniacs

Th**his** is a personal and anecdotal reflection on the men – they were always men – who not only owned newspapers but also loved to make news themselves: the proprietors. For most of the twentieth century, the stock notion of the major British newspaper proprietors was that they were megalomaniacs, or perhaps just plain maniacs. They were perceived, not least by the journalists who worked for them, as power-crazed, rumbustious, dangerous, even demonic figures. And the perception was valid. Many of the proprietors were indeed megalomaniacs.

The classic exemplar was Max Aitken, Lord Beaverbrook. An intelligent, charismatic and obsessively manipulative man, he was the son of a Scottish minister from Torphichen, near Bathgate, who had emigrated to Canada as a relatively young man. Beaverbrook arrived in Britain in 1910 and, for a complete outsider, penetrated the political and journalistic elites of London with extraordinary rapidity. He became Lloyd George's Minister for Information, and in 1919 he bought the *Daily Express*, which he made the most widely read daily paper in the world.

In the 1930s, Beaverbrook constantly attacked, through the *Express* and his other papers, Winston Churchill. Then he performed an amazing *volte-face*: he became Churchill's closest ally, and played his part in the winning of the Second

World War. He was Minister of Supply and evinced almost superhuman energy, for a man in his sixties, as he directed aircraft production. Yet Churchill's wartime deputy, Clement Attlee, described Beaverbrook in all seriousness as 'evil'.

In the 1920s and 1930s, Beaverbrook had built up his Express Group with bruising, blustering dynamism. Unlike his rival Lord Rothermere, Beaverbrook concentrated on just a handful of papers – notably the *Daily Express*, the *Evening Standard* and the *Scottish Daily Express*. Rothermere once announced bombastically that he intended to start new newspapers in Manchester, Sheffield, Bristol, Newcastle and Cardiff. Beaverbrook watched this project fail, and then cannily started his own paper – not in any of these cities, but in Glasgow. This was the *Scottish Daily Express*, first published in 1928. The *SDE* went on to become, in its brief but glorious life, the most remarkable phenomenon in Scottish newspaper history. Beaverbrook was an adventurer *par excellence*, and the *SDE* had a constant sense of adventure in its pages. (There is more about Beaverbrook in Chapter 7.)

But the proprietor who had the most direct influence on Scottish newspapers in the second half of the twentieth century was a very different animal, Roy Thomson. About all that he had in common with Beaverbrook was that he was a Canadian. Beaverbrook was not motivated by financial considerations: he was essentially a megalomaniac *journalist*, and he was prepared to throw money at his newspapers in defiance of all commercial convention. Thomson, on the other hand, was utterly uninterested in editorial matters, and he saw his newspapers as a means of making money. He was shrewd and canny, he was by no means an irresponsible proprietor, and many of his papers were quality products.

Thomson bought the *Scotsman*, for peanuts, in 1953; in 1959 he acquired the huge stable of Kemsley papers, including the *Aberdeen Press and Journal*; and in 1966 he bought the London *Times*. In 1964, he tried very hard to buy the *Glasgow*

Herald. In his offer, made formally to the board of George Outram & Co., the *Herald's* owners, Thomson indicated that urgent steps were needed to strengthen the national press of Scotland, particularly the quality newspapers. The offer document continued: 'The Directors of the Thomson Organisation further believe that the provision of first-class newspaper services and coverage in Scotland can best be achieved by aggressive development of these quality newspapers rather than by expansion of Scottish editions of English newspapers'. That, in the light of what has happened since, is a very significant quotation.

Roy Thomson failed to buy the *Herald* – and, in one sense, perhaps it is as well that he failed, for, after he died in 1976, the Thomson Organisation, and in particular Thomson Regional Newspapers, became notably less benevolent in their stewardship of their main Scottish titles, the *Scotsman* and the *Press and Journal*. But, in the 1950s and 1960s, Roy Thomson was good news, even if he himself was supremely uninterested in news. He was an unusual newspaper magnate in that he never sought to influence editorial policy. Indeed, he had a strong disdain for editorial matters. His principal interest was advertising; his preferred reading was balance sheets. He adored purchasing newspaper titles; it was almost as if he collected them. The American academic Stephen Koss, who was professor of history at Columbia University, New York, and a distinguished historian of the British press, wrote that Thomson regarded newspaper ownership 'not so much as a vocation as an addiction'.

Thomson was undoubtedly a benign influence at the *Scotsman*. He and his chosen editor Alastair Dunnett revived the paper throughout the 1950s and the 1960s. And, despite what I wrote above about Thomson not being interested in editorial matters, he did have the foresight to create two specialist training schools for graduates, to guide them through the interface between university and work at the

61

journalistic coalface. One of these was based in Newcastle, and I was one of the very first batch of trainees in 1969. We had already been hired by various Thomson papers (in my case the *Scotsman*), which we had visited briefly before going 'back to school' to learn the basics of newspaper journalism. There was huge competition for places at these training schools, and we regarded ourselves as a bit special – the chosen few.

At Newcastle, we were rapidly brought down to earth. We were taught by a couple of hard-bitten old pros who were not impressed by jumped-up young graduates with their high-falutin notions. We also had the opportunity to work on two excellent local papers, the *Newcastle Journal* and the *Newcastle Evening Chronicle*. I certainly benefited personally from this process, and I think it is fair to say that the British press has benefited generally from the specific journalistic training, geared for perhaps over-confident graduates, that Thomson had the foresight to provide.

He visited the Newcastle centre early in 1970, and I remember that he seemed an affable old cove. He was 75 then, with no side whatsoever and a frankly expressed belief that revenue was the key factor in the newspaper industry. He lectured us for about forty minutes on the importance of advertising, particularly classified as opposed to display advertising, and then took a few questions, which he answered with amiable blandness. Then he wished us well in our careers, and, after a breezy round of handshakes, he was gone.

It became the – in my opinion misguided – fashion to deride Thomson and to compare him unfavourably with more charismatic if less benign proprietors. People like Beaverbrook, and more recently Rupert Murdoch, may legitimately be regarded as not just all-powerful proprietors but also brilliant journalists. Thomson was no kind of journalist whatsoever. I sometimes felt that journalists who indulged in this derision for Thomson were ignorant, or stupid, or both. Surely it was refreshing to have a proprietor who showed scant interest in editorial policy, who allowed editors to get on and edit? My view is that, in some ways, Thomson was a refreshing change from politically obsessed proprietors like Beaverbrook who interfered constantly and obsessively in editorial matters.

One of Beaverbrook's finest editors, Ralph Blumenthal, opined in 1933 that the subordination of editors to proprietors was the principal change in newspapers in the early part of the twentieth century: 'Gone are the days when the Editor was the oracle whom no-one in or out of the office denied the right to print or omit what seemed best to him'. Well, I am certain that, in their long (seventeen-year) proprietor–editor working relationship, Roy Thomson never once treated Alastair Dunnett as anything other than the editorial oracle.

But Thomson's candid delight in making money and acquiring ever more newspapers did grate on the fastidious sensibilities of certain journalists. And the man could be crass, there is no doubt about that. In 1970, the year I encountered him in Newcastle, he gave a notorious television interview in which he was asked how many papers he owned. 'I think it's 182,' he said, 'but we bought one the other day in North Carolina, so that may make it 183.' He went on to say he'd like to own 365 papers – one for each day of the year. Needless to say, he did not achieve that particular ambition.

After Thomson died in 1976, the nature of his organisation changed. His son was a man of wider interests – he was a notable collector of fine art – and he too was a successful businessman. But he was more detached from his many newspapers, and he preferred to stay in his home town of Toronto. Various hard-headed executives – several of them former journalists – took increasing control of his UK newspaper interests, and the conduct of Thomson Regional

Newspapers was particularly problematic for the *Scotsman*. This paper's journalists rightly regarded it as a national, not a regional, title; the corollary was that it should be treated differently from titles like the *Newcastle Journal* and the *Aberdeen Press and Journal*, which were unashamedly regional in their ambitions and scope. This made life increasingly difficult for the editor of the *Scotsman* in the late 1970s and early 1980s, Eric Mackay, though for the most part he concealed his constant battles with the TRN management from his staff.

❛ ❜

The man who probably embodies the worst aspects of the megalomaniac proprietor was Ludvik Hoch, better known as Robert Maxwell. Born in a tiny Ruthenian village in the Czech Republic in 1923, he fought for the Allies in 1944 and 1945 with conspicuous valour. He was personally awarded the Military Cross by General Bernard Montgomery. This was the constant paradox of Maxwell. He was a man of terrific energy and courage; unfortunately, he all too often misdirected his exceptional personal qualities.

After the war, he founded Pergamon Press and developed many business interests in films, television, publishing and bookselling. He was a Labour MP from 1964 until 1970. At the time, it was occasionally asked how such a buccaneering and acquisitive capitalist managed to stand for election, and be elected, as a socialist; in a way, Maxwell was ahead of his time, and he anticipated what the Labour Party was to become. But few took him very seriously. Beaverbrook's *Sunday Express* described him as 'the biggest gasbag in the Commons'. He became a high-profile chairman of the Commons Catering Committee, firing staff and selling case after case of vintage wines. But what he really wanted to do was to run newspapers. Like many high-profile proprietors,

Maxwell was a man who combined colossal egotism with a kind of crazy chutzpah. But, unlike the really great interfering proprietors such as Beaverbrook and Murdoch, Maxwell had no editorial flair or judgment. And he was a crook.

Both of them had Herculean egos, but Beaverbrook's was more controlled, more subtle. His editors had a permanent instruction to publish any news about him – good or bad – whereas I should imagine that Maxwell would have been furious if any of his papers had printed anything negative about him. Beaverbrook could get on very well with other titanic figures such as Lloyd George and Churchill. Maxwell, on the other hand, was essentially a loner. And Beaverbrook was no mean historian, a man with a considerable understanding of the past. Maxwell had no sense of history.

❛ ❜

When the Beaverbrook flagship in Scotland, the *Scottish Daily Express*, finally failed in March 1974, brought down by union militancy as described in Chapter 6, Maxwell emerged as the *deus ex machina* who would salvage something from the wreckage. The last edition of the *SDE* appeared on 28 March, and thereafter more than 1,800 employees – including some of the best journalists in Scotland, and a few of the worst, as well as many experienced and skilled printers and compositors – found themselves on the streets. Among them was a small group who had the idea of a workers' paper, a title that would be called the *Scottish Daily News* and owned and managed by the employees. By no means all of them were the cream of the *SDE*. One or two of them were journalists who did not have the energy or talent to find work elsewhere; many of them were genuine idealists, happy to risk their redundancy money on a project they believed in.

And among their number was an exceptional man, Allister Mackie, a compositor in his early forties who emerged as a genuine leader. (That was part of the problem: newspapers require leadership; unlike some other businesses, it is difficult to run them as co-operatives, or by committee.) The ultimate irony was that these men, who wanted to run a democratic paper and were sick of proprietorial tyrants, ended up with the most monstrous proprietor of them all. The paper needed money, and Robert Maxwell was willing to provide it. But he was gross – physically huge, and grossly insensitive. His intervention turned out be catastrophic. Having put a considerable amount of cash into the new venture, Maxwell arrived at the old Express building in Albion Street, Glasgow, and immediately tried to take complete charge. He wanted to be the absolute boss. Within a fortnight, Mackie was challenging him and his seizure of full executive powers. This tension was reflected in the editorial failure of the paper.

Mind you, it had a bright start. In May 1975, the circulation rose to a splendid 330,000 copies. But, within weeks, it was collapsing. Eventually, in early August, the workers' council allowed Maxwell to assume formal control as chief executive. He moved a big – it must have been a very big – camp bed into Albion Street and took, literally, hands-on control. He even cooked meals in the canteen. But the irony was that a project conceived by the father of idealism and the mother of co-operation was now in the hands of someone who had a childish contempt for both qualities and who was at best an old-style press baron, at worst a diseased maniac. By September, the enterprise was in crisis. Mackie resigned, and Maxwell reigned supreme. But, although the circulation was maintained at around 150,000, even Maxwell could not save the paper. He resigned in October, despite the fact that most of the remaining workforce urged him to stay.

Scotland had not seen the last of him. Exactly a decade later, he seized, in an extraordinarily dramatic business coup, control of the huge Mirror Group in London. This organisation ran six major titles with a combined circulation of over 30 million a week. And two of the six were in Scotland: the country's best-selling tabloid, the *Daily Record*, and its sister paper the *Sunday Mail*. Maxwell was back. Before long, there was predictable turmoil at the *Record*'s high-rise headquarters on Anderston Quay, in the shadow of the Kingston Bridge on the north littoral of the Clyde in west Glasgow. Colin McClatchie, who was then a senior manager at the *Record*, recalls: 'Maxwell's style was very much: this is *my* business, this is *my* train set, and I will dictate what goes on. In some ways, decision-making was considerably shortened in that, if you wanted a decision, one person would make that decision and make it there and then.'

Maxwell had decided to take on both the journalists and the printers in what was to prove one of the most bitter newspaper disputes of the 1980s. He demanded a considerably longer working week and the unconditional introduction of new computerised printing and editorial technology. In the spring of 1986, matters came to a horrible head. Maxwell summarily ended a series of increasingly angry negotiations, decreed that well over 1,000 printers and journalists had dismissed themselves, and installed barbed wire round the plant to keep the workers out as the dispute grew ever more visceral. Eventually, Maxwell won; the unions accepted a cut of almost a third in the labour force and, even more humiliatingly, agreed to major changes in their working practices, more or less on Maxwell's terms.

Maxwell's death in 1991 was, in a grisly way, appropriate, for it combined drama, mystery and touch of black farce. He was found in the sea near the Canary Islands, having – apparently – slipped from his luxury yacht while taking a late-night pee over the side. Tributes were immediately paid to him by, among others, Charles Wilson, the distinguished Scottish journalist who was the editorial director of the Mirror Group when Maxwell died, and Helen Liddell, the Labour politician who had earlier been Maxwell's personnel and public-affairs director at the *Daily Record* (and is now Britain's High Commissioner in Australia). Some journalists were quick to attack these two for their tributes, given Maxwell's record; but he was in his own way a courageous man, always larger than life, always battling against the establishment, and many of his senior employees had a genuine respect for him despite the near-impossibility of working for him.

In the months after his death, however, the extent of his crookedness became all too apparent. He had been systematically siphoning large sums of money from his own companies, and robbing his employees' pension funds, in order to prop up his failing media empire. How criminality on this scale had been going on for so long, undiscovered, said much about the poor quality of accounting practice in Britain, as well as the poverty of investigative journalism.

' '

Early in 1981, I was hired by the aforementioned Charles Wilson as the sports editor on the paper he was launching in Glasgow, the *Sunday Standard*. This meant that my ultimate employer was another titan among capitalists, if a much more successful one than Maxwell – Rowland Furhop, better known as Tiny Rowland. He was chief executive of Lonrho, the trading conglomerate with substantial mining interests in Africa, which also owned a few newspapers into the bargain, including the *Glasgow Herald* and *Evening Times* and now the fledgling *Standard*. Rowland was an endlessly controversial figure, once pompously described by Ted

Heath as the unacceptable face of capitalism; but he was without doubt an acceptable and complaisant proprietor of the *Herald*.

The *Standard*, alas, failed. I switched to the *Herald*, eventually becoming deputy editor and, much later, editor. I arrived on the *Herald* floor shortly before the venerable paper celebrated its bicentenary, in 1983. The Queen visited the Albion Street offices – and, earlier that year, Margaret Thatcher, the prime minister, made a particularly memorable late-night visit in which many of those who met her, including myself, were drunk. (If the truth were told, she partook of a fair amount of whisky herself in the course of her visit.) Shortly before I and my colleague Ronnie Anderson met her, an officious executive complained to the editor, Arnold Kemp, that the two of us were so inebriated that we were in no fit state to be introduced to the nation's leader. Arnold, in his charming but firm way, brushed this officiousness aside. As it happened, I had bet my wife that I would kiss Mrs Thatcher's hand. I did so, and she had the grace to appear quite pleased as I slobbered over her rosy-pink fingers. Indeed, one witness claimed that she actually appeared highly delighted.

That night, she wooed most of the staff, and not just the newspaper staff. In the boardroom, she spent more time chatting with the waitresses than with the assembled VIPs. Throughout her visit, which lasted until well after midnight, twice as long as scheduled, she kept up a running banter with Michael Kelly, the then Lord Provost of Glasgow. Kelly gave as good as he got; it was that kind of occasion. When she arrived at the *Herald* picture desk, leading a straggling and increasingly rowdy entourage of journalists, executives and assorted hangers-on, she sat down, kicked off her shoes and loudly instructed the picture editor as to which were the best pictures on offer. The lady did not lack confidence. Although Thatcherism was deeply unpopular, especially in Glasgow, her ebullience combined with her friendly demeanour – her style was at once familiar and regal – seemed to win most of her detractors over as she progressed from floor to floor.

The Queen's visit, later in the year, was altogether more restrained. But the point of this is to note that the *Herald*'s owner, Tiny Rowland, never came near the paper in that memorable year. The head of state and the head of government found spaces in their crowded diaries to come to Glasgow and pay personal tribute to the 200-year-old *Herald* – but not the paper's proprietor, who had other priorities.

As long as the paper made money – and in the 1980s the *Herald*, always a profitable paper, did so spectacularly – Rowland left it well alone. It could be argued that at least some of the vast profit should have been ploughed back into the product for editorial development. It could certainly be argued that some of the paper's shareholdings in other media organisations – for example, its stake in Reuters, which Lonrho sold off for more than £10 million – should have been returned to the *Herald*; but Lonrho's stand-back ownership was perhaps a price well worth paying.

The editorial freedom we were allowed was precious. And, albeit after a considerable struggle, the managing director, the abrasive but far-sighted Terry Cassidy, was allocated the capital sum of £23 million to invest in new state-of-the-art colour printing presses and computerised technology, although even here Rowland and his buddies in the City drove a very hard bargain: they guaranteed the investment, but the *Herald* had to service the debt. And Cassidy, whose managerial style was combative to say the least, had resigned as managing director of Outram's well before he was able to enjoy the fruits of the new production facilities.

As for Arnold Kemp, he edited the *Herald* with flair and success for a full decade with Rowland as his proprietor – and he never once met the great man. Arnold often told me that he was curious to meet Rowland, yet some atavistic caution persuaded him that it was just as well that he didn't. There was only one occasion on which he had to rebuff a tentative attempt from Rowland to interfere editorially.

Of course, it would be ingenuous to be too starry-eyed about Rowland. He was also the owner of the *Observer*, and his stewardship of the London paper was much more capricious. At times, his performance as proprietor of that paper almost made Robert Maxwell look restrained. The *Herald*, 400 miles to the north, was not regarded as influential in areas that were important to him. It was profitable, seriously profitable, and he was content to leave well alone.

❝ ❞

In 1992, after several months of tortuous negotiations, Rowland sold the *Herald* to a management buy-out team led by Liam Kane, who had been installed as MD at Albion Street after a brief stint as the Herald Group's sales and marketing director. Before that, he had worked for both Murdoch and Maxwell in a high-flying newspaper management career that had taken him from Glasgow to London and back.

When the Kane buy-out was finally concluded, Arnold asked me to write a leader to mark the occasion. He gave me no further instructions. I wrote that the fact that the *Herald* and the *Evening Times* were returning to Scottish ownership was good news. 'There is a real sense of homecoming. A great Scottish institution is once again just that, in every sense.' But what proved surprisingly controversial was that I went on to note that it would be churlish not to mention the former owners. 'The international trading conglomerate, under the ever controversial but often inspired guidance of Tiny Rowland, has never been a favourite of the British establishment. But Lonrho never interfered with the *Herald*'s editorial content, and it was essentially a benign rather than a hostile proprietor.' This leader caused some eyebrows to raise, and Arnold was accused of sycophancy. He asked me, as its author, to respond to our critics, and I argued that it was hardly sycophantic to praise those who were no longer our owners, those to whom we were waving goodbye. What possible self-interest had we in being pleasant about those who no longer had any sway over us?

In a footnote to this episode, I should record that the leader was drawn to Rowland's attention at his headquarters in Cheapside, London. Rowland apparently studied it for some time and then inquired of an aide, with gentle puzzlement: 'My goodness, did we ask for this?' Even now, to write in generous terms about Lonrho's ownership of the *Herald* will be regarded by some as obsequious and servile. I utterly reject such criticism; mixed as the record of Lonrho may have been elsewhere, as far as the *Herald* was concerned, Lonrho's ownership was a period of prosperity and stability. And that was not a coincidence.

❛ ❜

The Liam Kane team had succeeded at precisely the wrong time. Britain's economy lurched from crisis to crisis in 1992. In September, there was a full-scale sterling crisis. The Chancellor, Norman Lamont, increased the base rate from 10 to 15 per cent in a desperate attempt to defend the pound against speculative selling by the likes of George Soros. The damage to business confidence was immense. Liam Kane later told me: 'We were afflicted, and I mean afflicted, by these very high interest rates. We'd a few other challenges, more than a few if the truth be told, but the high interest rates were the worst problem.'

Then Rupert Murdoch chose to start a price war in London. The consequences of this were many, and generally deleterious for the industry, if not its consumers (the consumers may be the most important consideration, but we should always remember also the shareholders and the employees). And London-based titles were increasingly flooding into Scotland, which was perceived as a soft market. Liam called this 'dumping' by multinational companies; shrewdly, he tried to play the Scottish card. Arnold backed him on this, but the relationship between the two extroverts was deteriorating. One of the problems was the fact that Liam had persuaded Arnold to change the paper's title to simply *The Herald*. The dropping of 'Glasgow' was agreed by Arnold, but driven by Liam. The logic was reasonable; the strategy was to build on the paper's success as a pan-Scotland title and to diminish its role as a city paper.

Yet Arnold was uneasy with the decision. He knew that the paper's relations with its home city were close and special (though, funnily enough, most of the complaints about the dropping of 'Glasgow' from the masthead came from far-flung readers). Arnold's unease came through in an interview he gave to Eddie Mair on Radio Scotland. Rightly or wrongly, Arnold convinced himself that Liam had manoeuvred him into a change that was against his better judgment. The other cause of lingering distrust was that Arnold himself was a leading member of the buy-out team. He was delighted and grateful that editorial independence was guaranteed during the buy-out negotiations, but he also felt slightly compromised.

So, it was a difficult time for Arnold. He was also bitterly disappointed with the general-election result in April 1992. He had been hoping for a Labour victory (which looked likely until the last minute) because he felt that it would pave the way for the eventual realisation of devolution. And, although he was personally friendly with various leading Scottish Tories, including Lord Macfarlane, George Younger, Malcolm Rifkind and the journalist Brian Meek, he had decided that he seriously disliked the actual party. He also remembered with distaste the hostile manoeuvres of certain Glasgow Tories when he had swung the *Herald* leftwards in the early 1980s. Thus, for various reasons, Arnold became troubled in the years after the tenth anniversary of his editorship, and his editorial touch became much less certain.

Meanwhile, as the price wars escalated, Conrad Black's *Daily Telegraph* responded to the way Murdoch had slashed the price of the *Times* by lowering its own cover price. The two titans, Murdoch and Black, were losing millions, though the most vulnerable title was the *Independent*. One of the adverse consequences that afflicted Liam Kane's always precarious strategy was that newspaper shares quickly became very dodgy propositions. And, of course, the intention of the team was that their buy-out vehicle, Caledonian Newspapers, should eventually be floated on the stock market.

As the UK economy struggled, the *Herald* just about held its own, but the *Evening Times* was in serious trouble; for every pound in profit the *Herald* made, the *Evening Times* lost 50p. Liam had to slash the Outram's payroll by almost 400. He managed to do this without an industrial dispute; he was an effective, and consistently charming, negotiator. Even more controversially, the (generous) working conditions for all staff were rendered much more harsh. It was a period of consolidation, cutbacks, perpetual tension and increasing concern about the future of both titles. Liam somehow held the project together with his constant availability – for once, the phrase 'my door is always open' was accurate – his amiability and his patent personal commitment to the cause.

It was an exceptionally exciting period, at once invigorating and alarming. Liam held journalists in high esteem – he reckoned that they tended to be more intelligent than managers are, and their only problem was what he called an inbuilt arrogance – and he undoubtedly presided over considerable increases in editorial pagination on both titles. Any objective outsider could have seen that the two titles were actually receiving more investment after the buy-out; but there was some sniping from other newspaper houses. Liam says he still resents that, to this day. He thinks that the *Sunday Times Scotland* and *Scotland on Sunday* were the two main culprits. Ian Bruce, who was the journalists' leader on the *Herald* at the time, recalls Liam as a man 'who at heart was a newspaperman. As far as I can remember, he never lost a day's production, though some entire departments vanished, virtually overnight. Liam was always approachable, and he was OK to deal with. But some of the managers he brought in weren't so savvy. In fact, there was a fly-by-night feel about some of them.'

Liam sent several executives, including myself, to a series of specially structured management courses held over several weekends at Troon, of all places. (The hotel was first-class – and, perhaps as a recompense for our giving up not one but three weekends, we were allowed to run up huge wine bills.) What surprised me then, and surprises me to this day, was that there was no special emphasis on industrial relations in these intensive weekend sessions. That the *Herald* and the *Evening Times* managed to survive the early 1990s without a major industrial dispute is, in retrospect, almost beyond belief.

But the stresses of that period took their toll. Albion Street always seemed to be awash with drink, but I recall that period as being particularly boozy. Increasingly, Liam had to work eighteen-hour days in his attempts to keep the three main banking backers on board. And Liam and Arnold were, in terms of their working relationship, at breaking point. One night, Arnold was so angered by Liam's performance at an earlier fractious meeting that he told me in all seriousness that he was returning to the office to 'kill' Liam. I had physically to restrain him from leaving the pub (inevitably, we were in the pub). I am not making this up.

Eventually, and very sadly, Liam decided he had no option but to fire Arnold. One of the finest editorships in the history of the Scottish press had ended in precisely the wrong way. Liam brought in, as the new editor of the *Herald*, George McKechnie, who had edited the *Evening Times* for twelve years. George was at once more abrasive and more pliant than Arnold. It was an incredibly sensitive time, and George was received on the *Herald* with considerable suspicion, not least because he immediately got rid of five of the paper's most senior journalists. I had offered my resignation when Arnold was fired. Liam insisted that I stay on, but I was uneasy about continuing as George's deputy. George assured me that he wanted me to provide continuity and to help to ease him into his new role. I too was suspicious. But I quickly realised that he was a very hard-working and thoughtful editor. More surprisingly, he proved to be kind and sensitive in his dealings with his staff, though if he reads those words he will resent them, as he always cultivated a brusque, even boorish, hard-man persona.

Eighteen months later, in the summer of 1996, it finally became clear that the management buy-out was in need of fresh outside help. The stock market was in turmoil (in one three-week period, it went down 15 per cent). Liam searched for a white knight, and that elusive figure finally emerged in the guise of STV (formerly Scottish Television) led by the chairman Gus Macdonald, his chief executive Andrew Flanagan, and the finance director Gary Hughes. Liam says that he was very happy with STV: 'They had the back-up resources we simply didn't have'. STV paid £105 million for the two papers.

When the deal was eventually clinched, the closing mechanics were attended to in a way that was, in the manner of modern business, brutal. Several key executives in the buy-out team were asked to leave the building immediately and to hand in their company-car keys before they did so. Ron Macdonald, the financial director, refused to do so; he wanted to drive home with dignity and return his car later. Liam's team had struggled valiantly to sustain what was perhaps, with the advantage of hindsight, always a doomed enterprise. Liam Kane, in particular, had laboured night and day for over four years to make his dream come true. He had lost a great editor and had demanded a lot of blood, sweat and tears. The effort had been almost superhuman.

"

The lessons of all this are, I suspect, that newspapers are best run by big organisations. A very small executive team, in thrall to the banks and stretched by the need to try to micromanage on a daily basis as well as deal with strategic planning and complex financial negotiations, was always going to be desperately overstretched. And, if the wider economic climate was unpropitious, as it most certainly was between 1992 and 1996, it was inevitable that sooner or later everything would implode. The big groups, even the mid-sized ones, have the muscle and the manpower to compete as the market gets ever more competitive. Liam's buy-out was predicated on the market remaining more or less as it was in 1991–2, which, looking back, was a period of near-innocence.

George McKechnie stayed on for a month or so, but he disliked the minute scrutiny that was now being applied to all aspect of editorial spending. Liam had, in fact, treated us journalists with almost excessive respect. Now everything had to be justified, down to the finest detail. Right at the start of 1997, George told me privately that he could not work with Gus and his colleagues. A fortnight later, he resigned. Two days later, Gus summoned me to his office in Cowcaddens and weighed me up. I told him that I had loyally and to the best of my ability served two *Herald* editors over a long period; I felt I did not have it in me to serve a third. If I did not get the job, I'd leave. Gus said frankly that he'd take his time in assessing me, and that he'd have a good look at various other candidates. But he indicated that I was in pole position, and did give me the welcome assurance that if I did go, he'd make sure the deal was as generous as he could possibly make it.

A few weeks later, I was confirmed as editor. I had worked very closely with Arnold and then George, but I was now to experience directly what they had both warned me about: an editor has to spend an enormous amount of time not on journalism but on management. He, or she, straddles an uneasy halfway house between editorial – which is what he or she is supposed be good at – and the territory of the proprietor, which tends to be financial. Proprietors like Beaverbrook, who were prepared to take a cavalier attitude to editorial expenditure, and were more interested in editorial than commercial matters, are but a distant, if fond, memory.

Along with the managing editor of the Herald Group, Bob Jeffrey, I endured a series of almost comically fraught negotiations with Andrew Flanagan and Gary Hughes. The management of the paper became much more focused; the attention to detail was rigorous. We had to make draconian cuts, but it had been agreed that there would be no compulsory redundancies; this was my own bottom line. Gary regularly annoyed me by insisting that, as far as he was concerned, I was not a journalist at all. I was a manager, and furthermore a manager who was responsible for an editorial budget of around £10 million.

Although I found Andrew and Gary hard taskmasters on the financial front, they were exemplary in their restraint and indeed their understanding when it came to editorial matters. The one thing we could not achieve was more 'synergy' with the television operations. (Shortly after Scottish acquired the *Herald*, they bought Grampian Television.) For one reason or another, newspapers and television are very different worlds, beset by mutual suspicion. In the summer of 1999, when the *Herald* was placed under sustained and, in my view, quite vicious political pressure, Andrew Flanagan's quiet support, and that of the man he had appointed as managing director of the newspaper division, Des Hudson, were invaluable and much appreciated. All in all, I was incredibly lucky in my career; I never once experienced direct editorial interference by an owner.

In a footnote to all this, it was early in 2003 that the Scottish Media Group (formerly Scottish Television) sold the *Herald* titles to Newsquest, the UK subsidiary of a major US media concern, Gannett. The selling price was £216 million – not bad when you consider that the same business had been bought by Liam Kane and his team for £93 million just eleven years earlier, and even more impressive if you think that Scottish paid just £105 million for the business in 1996. The SMG management had certainly added value; and, to their enormous credit, they had launched the *Sunday Herald* in 1999. Unlike the *Sunday Standard* eighteen years earlier, the *Sunday Herald* was carefully planned. It soon established itself commercially as well as editorially. This was particularly impressive, as *Scotland on Sunday*, launched by the Scotsman Group in 1988, was now well established as a pan-Scotland quality paper. (Or, to look at it another way, the *Sunday Standard* had failed when it had the field to itself; the *Sunday Herald* was launched in the face of a young but already strong competitor.) I trust that I played at least some part in building the value of the group, although by 2003 I had been away for a couple of years, and I did not benefit personally from the sale. But I've no regrets about that. The

Herald, whose survival had been in doubt in 1996, was, for the time being anyway, safe and well, even if it would not necessarily survive for another two centuries.

❝ ❞

Not all newspaper owners are flamboyant, larger-than-life figures like Beaverbrook, Maxwell or Murdoch. For a few troubled years in the late 1990s and the early part of the twenty-first century, the Scotsman Group in Edinburgh was owned by the hyper-reclusive Barclay Brothers. Almost as reclusive are the Thomson family, who own DC Thomson in Dundee. After years of lying even lower than usual, DC Thomson suddenly purchased the *Aberdeen Press and Journal* and the *Evening Express*, early in 2006, for £132 million.

DC Thomson had presided over the spectacular decline of their most famous title, the *Sunday Post*. In the twenty years from 1985 to 2005, this paper's circulation dropped by more than one million. In other words, it managed to lose three million readers, if the customary rule of three readers per copy sold is applied. This appalling loss reflected sociological and cultural change as much as editorial malfunction: the couthy *Sunday Post* will be forever associated with a homely, pawky, kailyard idea of Scotland. That version of Scotland was maybe appropriate in the 1950s and even to some extent in the 1960s and 1970s, but has now gone forever. In one sense, it is to the company's credit that they did not try to reinvent the title. And, to be fair to DC Thomson, their stewardship of the redoubtable Dundee morning paper, the *Courier*, has been much more effective.

DC Thomson's purchase of the *P&J* perhaps indicates a renewed interest in newspapers. For some time, the company had been making most of its money out of investments other than newspapers. In the year to March 2005, its pre-tax profit was £43 million, but its trading profit was only £10 million. A much bigger player in the newspaper industry is the Edinburgh-based Johnston Press, which acquired the Scotsman Group in 2005 for around £160 million. This company now owns over 300 titles. Led by the canny yet acquisitive chief executive Tim Bowdler, it is probably the company to watch in terms of future developments in Scottish newspaper ownership. Johnston Press's pre-tax profits in the calendar year 2005 were £151 million.

Of the five great Scottish indigenous daily titles, the *Record*, the *Herald*, the *P&J*, the *Courier* and the *Scotsman*, the last three are now safely in Scottish hands. One thing is certain: none of these five titles is run by old-fashioned, journalistically inclined, rumbustious proprietors of the cast of Beaverbrook. The last of that breed is Rupert Murdoch, and he of course owns the *Scottish Sun*.

4

Scotland's Best Newspaper

Arrogant, adroit and audacious, the *Scottish Daily Express* was a phenomenon to behold. In its glory years – from the mid-1950s to the early 1970s, when it was tragically brought down by myopic industrial militancy – it was Scotland's finest paper. Not the most influential, or august, or serious paper – but just the best.

It is in a way peculiar that I should be writing that. Most Scottish journalists of my vintage – those born before 1950 – are neatly divided into two camps: those who worked for the *Express* in its pomp, and those who didn't. Almost all those who worked for it venerate its memory. I recall the late Brian Meek, politician, pressman and emphatically not a man of sentiment, speaking of the great days of the *Express* in a most maudlin manner. Yet, too many of those who didn't work for it sneer at it to this day. I put this down to simple envy. I never worked for the *SDE*, but I hope I am broad-minded enough to appreciate the glorious memory of its constant remorseless energy, its swagger and style and flair, and its occasional effrontery.

It might be perverse to illustrate the *SDE*'s excellence by digging up an episode from the arts world, not always an area where the *Express* was reckoned to excel. But here, as in so many other spheres, it made a consistently meaningful impact. In 1967, the reinvigorated Scottish National Orchestra went on an extended inaugural tour of Europe, starting in Austria, moving on through Germany and ending up in the Netherlands. The audiences were enthusiastic as the orchestra progressed through some of the world's finest concert halls. The tour was a triumph. It was, in its way, historic. Among other things, the tour was the making of the orchestra's young maestro, Alex Gibson.

The only journalist to cover the full three weeks of the tour was Conrad Wilson of the *Scotsman*, but the opening concerts were also covered by another Scottish staffer, Neville Garden, the music critic of the *Scottish Daily Express*. Conrad recalls: 'It is to the immense credit of the *Express* that they sent Neville to the opening concerts in Vienna. Neville actually filed more copy than I did in those early days of the tour, covering all aspects, even a bout of food poisoning among some of the players, and not just the opening concerts. As for the *Glasgow Herald*, it just wasn't interested. You could say that at that time the only two papers which took the performing arts in Scotland seriously were the *Scotsman* and the *Express*.'

Magnus Magnusson, who worked in the Edinburgh office of the *Scottish Daily Express* in the early 1960s, reminisces about the chief reporter in that branch office. 'His name was Gilbert Cole, and he was a far more cultured and cultivated man than one would have expected to be on the *Scottish Daily Express*. But the *Express* was in fact full of extremely cultivated people, and it belied its retrospective reputation that it was just a tabloid, which of course it was not, in those days anyway. No, it was a broadsheet, and it took itself very seriously. We didn't, but the paper did.'

❝ ❞

The *Express* was not too bothered about the *Scotsman* or the *Glasgow Herald* or even the *Scottish Daily Mail*. Its great and constant rival was a real tabloid, the *Daily Record*. Murray Ritchie joined the *Record* as a reporter in 1965, from the *Dumfries and Galloway Standard*. He arrived in Glasgow, a fresh-faced 24-year-old, and was immediately pitched into the most intense and visceral rivalry there has ever been in the Scottish newspaper history. 'There was this tremendous, unrestrained, freebooting rivalry. We were taught, even brainwashed, to treat the *Express* as the enemy; and to this day I have an irrational dislike of the *Scottish Daily Express*', recalls Ritchie.

The *Record* had the staff to cover the big stories with squads of reporters, yet somehow the *Express* always had more manpower. Ritchie remembers one of his early experiences. 'It was, in a way, a classic story from those days, a big fire at the Odeon cinema in Renfield Street, Glasgow. The *Record* had several reporters on the spot within minutes of hearing about it, but there were plenty of *Express* guys there too, and more and more and more of them kept arriving. They just kept coming. They came in private cars, hire cars, taxis, they jumped out of trolley buses … the story in the *Express* the next day had ten bylines on it, but there were far more than ten reporters actually there. And they had a squad of photographers there too. Looking back, I have to admit that the *Express* had this terrific sense of simply being – big. They seemed to have this huge staff and limitless resources. They would swarm around, talking to everyone and trying to cover every possible angle. The *Express* seemed to be everywhere and to look into everything, and it was involved in all aspects of Scottish life. Whereas the *Record* – and I really enjoyed working on it, don't get me wrong – was more the cheeky wee tabloid, the working man's paper.'

Ritchie recalls that although – because? – the *Express* had superior resources, the *Record* staff were prepared to play dirty to beat the *Express*. 'There would be car chases across Glasgow; and, if you got into a phone box – no mobile phones then – before the guys from the *Express*, you would try to cut the wires so that they couldn't use the phone. There was a certain amount of piracy. For a young guy entering journalism, it was a very steep and quite alarming learning curve at times.' Fidelma Cook, who also worked on the *Record*, remembers: 'We had professional drivers who would take us around, and when they could they would open the bonnets of the *Express* cars and take out vital bits so that they wouldn't start up'.

It would be wrong to suggest that the *Record* was in any sense under-resourced. Harry Conroy, who went on to be both a fine financial journalist and the UK leader of the journalists' union, the NUJ, remembers his first experience of covering a major disaster for the *Record*. Late one night in 1965, a BEA Vanguard crashed in fog while trying to land at London after a flight from Edinburgh. Conroy, along with many other *Record* reporters, was hauled from his bed as the full extent of the disaster became known. He was sent to Renfrew Airport (as it then was), where BEA officials were expected to release the names of those victims who had been identified. Conroy, then aged 22, was one of the most junior of the *Record* team covering the disaster in London, Edinburgh, Glasgow and Dundee. Altogether, the *Record* mustered a reporting team of eighteen. But one thing is certain: the *Express* would have had even more personnel covering the story.

❝ ❞

The rivalry was less evident in the capital, where things were generally much more douce. The *Record* was not very high-profile; at jobs where you would encounter two or three *Express* reporters, quite often there was no-one from the *Record*. When I was working as a reporter on the *Scotsman* in the early 1970s, my colleagues and I knew that the *Express* Edinburgh office, just 200 yards away in Jeffrey Street, had more than twice the number of reporters that we had in our head-office newsroom. In some ways, this indicated the less attractive side of the *Express*, for many of these reporters did not have enough to do. There was an element of sitting around waiting for the big story – usually a disaster of some kind – to break.

Some of these reporters were very sharp and hungry, but not all of them. One or two of them carried a slight undertone of bitterness; they sensed that they were missing out on the big time. Glasgow was very much the place to be. Reporters in Edinburgh sometimes spoke of the city in the west in tones of sheer awe. Furthermore, newspaper branch offices are not always good places in which to work. Altogether, there was far less of the frenetic, piratical, cut-throat mentality in Edinburgh. As well as a huge number of reporters, the *Scottish Daily Express* also employed many sportswriters and an amazing complement of twenty-two feature-writers. The paper carried only two or three daily features slots, yet somehow it managed to keep these writers – who included outstanding journalists such as Deirdre Chapman, Brian Meek, Mamie Baird, Charles Graham and Jack Webster – happy. The good pay helped.

‘’

The man who was to become the lead feature-writer on the *Scottish Daily Express*, Jack Webster, had joined the paper in 1960. He began his career on the *Turriff Advertiser* and moved on to the *Press and Journal* in Aberdeen. He recalls arriving in the large open-plan editorial floor of the *Express* in that famous building in Albion Street, Glasgow, nicknamed the ‘black Lubyanka’. In the *P&J* offices in Broad Street, Aberdeen, the reporters and sub-editors had worked on different floors in small rooms, and the editorial team was literally compartmentalised.

In Albion Street, everything was noisily, feverishly different. There was 'a buzz of vitality' which, according to Webster, typified the spirit of Glasgow itself. He observed the shirt-sleeved executives on the news desk conducting 'a kind of frenetic performance of newsgathering which owed at least something to Hollywood and must have done more for the adrenaline than it did for the nervous system'. The quasi-American bravado was not confined to the journalists. Webster recalls that the man who had the contract for the *Express*'s large fleet of private cars was a character called Eddie McKenna, who operated from a hut across Albion Street from the *Express* building. 'Eddie McKenna exemplified the swagger. He had this big broad-brimmed hat; he looked like someone from Chicago. Beaverbrook employed him to organise not just the transport but all the vendors through the city. He smoked big cigars, and he had style.'

Webster's first shift, in February 1960, ran from 6pm until 2am. He can still remember it as if it were yesterday: a bustling, tiring, smoke-filled night that hovered forever between excitement and hysteria as editions were either caught or missed. Webster was working as a sub-editor, and he soon realised that, despite all the bravura and puffed-up self-importance, the actual standards of copy he was subbing fell somewhat short of the quality he had known on the *P&J*. So, he began submitting the occasional article to the *Express* features department; before too long, he had become a full-time feature-writer.

The *Express* then was obsessed with celebrity, but the difference from much present-day journalism is that their celebrities were genuine and established, not trivial, fleeting, fifteen-minute celebrities. I remember Brian Meek telling me how nervous and awestruck he was before interviewing Sir Stanley Matthews, possibly England's finest-ever footballer, for the *SDE* – and how impressed he was with the man's modesty, courtesy and quiet reflectiveness. Among those whom Jack Webster interviewed exclusively for the *Scottish Daily Express* were Bing Crosby and Charlie Chaplin. He also brought the great Muhammad Ali to Albion Street, where Ali actually took over – briefly – from the editor Ian McColl, sitting in the editor's chair and masterminding the lunchtime editorial conference.

Jack's account of how, after pursuing Chaplin off and on for five long years, he eventually persuaded the great man to grant him an interview is a tale that says much about both the *Express*'s resources and that rare but important journalistic virtue, perseverance. Chaplin, by far the greatest star of the silent-movie era, was still an authentic world figure. But he was reclusive. He enjoyed taking the occasional hyper-discreet holiday in Scotland. He lived in Switzerland, having moved there from California after being persecuted for his left-wing views. He had a strong and justified suspicion of journalists.

Jack had received a tip that Chaplin and his wife Oona – daughter of the great playwright Eugene O'Neill – were taking a holiday in Scotland for the first time in several years. He had been told by a contact in the North-East that they were secretly booked into the Tor-na-Coille, a stylish but by no means palatial hotel that was situated on the western outskirts of the Deeside town of Banchory. The hotel refused to confirm that the Chaplins were coming, so Jack simply booked himself in and then sat in the foyer reading books, drinking cocktails and coffee and hoping that the limousine would duly appear. And one day it did.

He observed the Chaplins having dinner before he approached Oona. She was not especially helpful, telling Jack: 'Well, you know what he feels about journalists'. Jack replied that he was not on a witch-hunt but was 'just somebody wanting to write an article about a hero'. The next morning, Oona told Jack that Chaplin would not change his mind. But Jack had a little trick. He had Chaplin's autobiography with him. He approached the great man and asked him to sign it. Then he asked for autographs for his three sons. He noticed that Chaplin did not just sign his name but also added, beside each signature, a little sketch of himself, complete with the bowler hat, the baggy breeks and the stick. So, while Chaplin was working on the little drawings, Jack took the opportunity, gently, to begin asking questions. And then he produced his masterstroke. He said to Chaplin: 'Back about 1906, you appeared at the Tivoli in Aberdeen?'

Chaplin replied: 'Yes, that was just before Stan Laurel and I went off to America'. So, Jack then asked: 'How would you like to see the old place? It's still there, a bingo hall now.' Chaplin replied that he'd quite like that. So, he spoke to his chauffeur – and Charlie, Jack and Oona drove into Aberdeen. Jack recalls: 'Suddenly, he began to loosen up. I think he began to realise that at that stage in his life there was no great ill in speaking to a guy like me.' Jack managed to make frantic contact with an *Express* photographer in Aberdeen, and the precious moment at the Tivoli was recorded in image as well as words. And he had achieved his aim: a comprehensive, candid interview with the very first cinematic superstar.

I record that story at some length because it is a useful counterpoint to all the wild tales of derring-do and dirty tricks in Glasgow. The *Express* truly had a range, a gamut of stories and of styles: it could scrap in the gutter if need be, or it could tease out reminiscences from the greatest cinematic genius in history, or it could report on concerts from the glittering halls of European capitals. In its heyday, it reached a circulation of more than 650,000, about 200,000 ahead of the *Record*. These are extraordinary figures. The received circulation rule is that for every paper sold, there will be three readers. So, these two papers were then reaching out to well over three million in a country of just five million people.

In the 1930s, in the first decade of its existence, the *Scottish Daily Express* had been less dominant. Indeed, in 1939, Beaverbrook's general manager in Scotland, the astute Frank Waters, held discussions with Beaverbrook about launching a serious bid for either the *Scotsman* or the *Glasgow Herald*. Waters noted that, in London, people spoke in terms of reverence about these two papers. Though they were rarely read in England, they enjoyed a very high reputation. But Beaverbrook decided instead to concentrate on developing the *Scottish Daily Express*, and, after the war, he poured more and more money into it. Jack Webster says: 'Although the *Scottish Daily Express* could take copy from the big *Express* bureaux in Washington and New York and Europe, and could use the big byline writers working for the *Express* in London, it was very much a Scottish paper. There was a growing need to beat the *Record*. And the *Record* wasn't a bad paper, but it looked cheaper than the *Express*, it looked just a little tacky.'

❝❞

When I was growing up in Aberdeen in the 1950s, my family, Glaswegian exiles, took two papers: the *Glasgow Herald* and the *P&J*. The *Herald* was a given; it was a statement, as much as anything else, about our Glasgow provenance. But then, I think in the late 1950s, the *P&J* was dropped and we started getting the *Scottish Daily Express* instead. (We still saw the *P&J*. My father got the *P&J* at his bank, where he was manager, and sometimes remembered to bring it home.) The decision to drop the local paper and switch to the *Express* was, I think, taken at the time of the trial of Peter Manuel at the High Court in Glasgow (see Chapter 7). The *SDE* covered this extraordinary trial in exhaustive detail.

I remember that my mother had a particular fondness for the *Express*; it was a paper that always had a special appeal for female readers, partly because it never ignored the softer aspects of the news agenda, and because it employed an impressive array of female writers. Among them were the aforementioned Mamie Baird and Deirdre Chapman, and others such as Sheila McNamara, Lorna Rhind, Lorna Blackie and Molly Kelly. To say that the *SDE* appealed to women is not to make a sexist point. Rather, it is to note that, in those days, when too much journalism was macho, hard-bitten, blood-on-the-streets stuff about crime and disaster, the *Express* was broad-minded enough to understand that there was another, gentler constituency.

At this time, many households did not have a television set. Newspapers were an essential source of both information and entertainment. I started to read through the *Express* every day, marvelling at its gusto and its constant readability. The other papers I'd sampled were not like this at all. There was nothing pompous or stern about it. One of my school pals was Neil Borthwick, whose dad ran the *Express* bureau in Aberdeen. From Neil, I heard various stories of this peculiar world of newspapers, at once raffish and glamorous and slightly surreal. It was round about then that I decided I wanted to be a journalist.

I cannot actually remember the most famous of all the *Express* campaigns, which was to prevent the imposition of bishops by the Church of Scotland, mooted by a Kirk committee in 1958. The *Express*, true to Beaverbrook's Presbyterian soul, ran features of supercharged indignation which are still talked about, almost fifty years later, with awe. The *Express* was not a 'paper of record'. It had plenty of news, but it was an issue-driven paper. It preferred, if possible, to make its own news.

The *Scottish Daily Express*'s finest editor was Ian McColl, who, Jack Webster reckons, was Beaverbrook's all-time favourite editor, above even Ralph Blumenthal and Arthur Christiansen. The proprietor rarely visited the Albion Street plant, but he was on the phone to McColl every evening.

❛ ❜

The *Scottish Daily Express* deployed enormous power and influence, not least in the world of sport. Jack Webster was involved in one of the paper's sporting coups when, in 1964, the *SDE* hit on a stunt involving the most celebrated football coach of that era, Helenio Herrera of Inter Milan. The idea was born not on the sports desk but, like many of the best journalistic ideas, in the features department. The features editor, Drew Rennie, told Jack to get himself to Italy as quickly as possible to make contact with Herrera. (Rangers had been drawn against Inter Milan in the European Cup.)

The idea was that Jack would gain Herrera's confidence and persuade him to let Jack 'ghost' a series of pieces by Herrera on Rangers in particular and Scottish football in general. It was Jack's first, but by no means last, experience of being told to grab his passport and some currency and catch a plane at very short notice. Jack met the redoubtable coach, persisted in their halting, awkward conversations and eventually negotiated a deal. The best part of the stunt was the follow-up. The *Express* offered any football manager in Scotland the chance to fly to Italy and spend a week studying the methods of the man who was then the leading coach in the world.

Jack takes up the story: 'So, we offered this opportunity to every Scottish manager and his coach, trainer as it then was, and yet only two Scottish managers took it up. One was Jock Stein, who was with Dunfermline before moving briefly to Hibs and then of course on to Celtic, and the other was Willie Waddell, who was manager of Kilmarnock. The two of them and their coaches spent a full week with Herrera, as promised. Herrera won the European Cup with Inter Milan over the next two years. But look what happened to our two managers who had the vision and imagination to take up the *Express* offer. Waddell proceeded to win the Scottish League with Kilmarnock in 1965. Jock Stein won the league with Celtic in 1966, and they went on to win the European Cup in 1967, the first British team to do so. So, once again, the *Express* was able to say – our boys did it! And that was exactly the mentality of the *Express*.'

In a postscript to that anecdote, it was a few years later that the *Express* signed Willie Waddell to join its already vast staff of full-time sportswriters. (I remember, as a teenager in Aberdeen in the early 1960s, being surprised that the *Express* retained a full-time football writer in Aberdeen, a man called Ronnie Main, whose only remit was to cover Aberdeen Football Club. At that time, AFC were in the doldrums, but that did not matter to the *Express*. Even more remarkably, the *Express* employed a full-time Highland football correspondent, based in Inverness.) Waddell, whose writing was as abrasive as his wing play for Rangers had been scintillating, wrote a series of devastatingly critical articles attacking the Ibrox club's new manager, the relatively young and inexperienced Davie White. Waddell nastily christened him 'the boy David'. Not surprisingly, White found himself out of a job. That was the power of the *Express*. And his replacement as Rangers manager was none other than Willie Waddell.

Of course, it was not to last. The dramatic story of how the *SDE* was brought down by union militants is told in Chapter 6. The end came in March 1974. Jack Webster remembers: 'It was the most amazing night. Grown men were weeping. I mean, people who had spent their lives there. I was choked up myself, and I knew that here was the *Express* that had employed 2,000 people in Scotland, and

1,800 of those people were going to be out on the street. It was such a sad business. We were out there in Albion Street, and we were looking at the great black glass building, and we thought: this is the end, our paper has gone …'

( )

But the demise of the *Scottish Daily Express* meant an opportunity for the *Record*. It had lost its protracted and bitter circulation battle with the *SDE*, but had never given up. It yapped and snarled at the *Express*. It was a persistent wee terrier of a paper, a fighter. And it may not have won the war, but it won plenty of skirmishes.

In 1967, Winnie Ewing, a glamorous young Glasgow solicitor, won the Hamilton by-election for the Scottish National Party. The word 'sensational' is overused in journalism, but this was an authentically sensational political event. It was a seminal moment in modern Scottish life. Through in Edinburgh, Alastair Dunnett pondered on the significance of the result and decided to embark on his crusade for devolution. In Glasgow, the *Express* and the *Record* scrambled to sign up Winnie Ewing for a weekly column. Significant sums were thrown at her. Senior figures in the SNP advised her to choose the *Record*, as it was a Labour paper, and the Nationalists needed Labour votes.

Ewing recalls that she could not write the way the *Record* wanted, so one of the paper's feature-writers was appointed as her 'ghost'. He was Mike Grieve, son of the poet Hugh MacDiarmid, arguably Scotland's greatest creative genius of the twentieth century, and the husband of one of the *Express*'s star writers, Deirdre Chapman. Scotland is a small country.

( )

So, from the spring of 1974, the *Record* had a clear run. The opportunity was seized with panache by Bernie Vickers, an Englishman who was eccentric, to put it mildly, but nonetheless a brilliant if wayward *Record* editor, and by his successor, the shrewd but much less ebullient Dundonian Endell Laird. Soon, the *Record* was adding literally hundreds of thousands to its circulation without, it seemed, a rival in sight. Joan Burnie, who was the paper's agony aunt, recalls Vickers as one of the truly great editors. 'He could see the talent in people, and he knew how to use it. That is perhaps the most important gift in an editor. For example, he turned John Fairgrieve, who'd been a sportswriter with the *Scottish Daily Mail*, into an outstanding pundit and feature-writer.'

Jack Irvine, who was working as a senior production journalist on the *Record* at this time, recalls: 'There was relentless pressure in producing the *Record*. You spent the early afternoon through to the early evening running the first edition together, and would close copy at about 8:30pm. And, immediately you'd done that, you would then start work on different editions for Edinburgh, and the Borders, and various other regions, for Dundee, Aberdeen etc. etc. In those days, there was a full-scale ripping-out of stories to put in local stories for each area, and that's why the *Record* sold so well, because it editionised. Unfortunately, as costs started to bite and new managements came, they took the view that all this was terribly expensive. The irony has been that, although technology came on in leaps and bounds, the service the papers are actually providing has got lesser and lesser.'

Nonetheless, the *Record*'s sales rose relentlessly. By 1984, ten years after the fall of the *SDE*, it was selling more than 750,000. But there were clouds on the horizon. Robert Maxwell, that most megalomaniac of proprietors, had bought Mirror Group Newspapers, the *Record*'s owners. Soon he was at war with his staff, and there was a long and debilitating strike. Joan Burnie recalls: 'Bernie Vickers had gone, and the place became much more divisive. Those who hadn't gone on strike were rewarded with promotions. They were given executive positions. This had a very bad effect on morale.'

❛ ❜

The *Record* had competed vigorously with the *Scottish Daily Express*, and had lost. Then there was a long period in which the *Record* had no meaningful rival. But, when a new rival emerged, in the saucy shape of Rupert Murdoch's *Scottish Sun*, history repeated itself. Once again, the *Record* struggled when faced with hungry, zestful and direct competition.

Murdoch, the most brilliant and ruthless proprietor since Beaverbrook, saw in his *Sun* the chance to take on the *Record*. And so, for almost twenty years, the *Scottish Sun* and the *Daily Record* have been locked in a debilitating and bitter battle. At the time of writing (mid-2006), the circulations are within a few thousand of each other: the *Record* is at just over 400,000 and the *Sun* at just under 400,000. The gap is about 30,000. This is remarkable because, as recently as ten years ago, the *Record* was selling more than 750,000. The reality is that the *Record* has not really understood how to compete with the brash, bruising momentum of the *Sun*.

The *Record* used to be a serious newspaper, whereas Murdoch's *Sun* is, above all, cheeky. Indeed, it is part-comic, part-newspaper. It is relentlessly, gloriously mischievous. It has a downmarket brio that is alien to its rival's traditions. It is unashamedly fascinated by excess and scandal and consumption, the more conspicuous the better. In the traditional sense of newspapers, it is an outsider, the irrepressible new kid on the block. In other words, it presents a colossal challenge for the *Record*; and the *Record*'s response has not been consistent. To put it bluntly, the *Record* has never known whether to try to take on the *Sun* at its own game, or to stay aloof and position itself marginally upmarket.

My personal view is that the *Record* should have made clear from the start of the extended battle that it was a heavier, more serious paper, staying faithful to its traditions of the 1950s, 1960s and 1970s. But to write that is easy enough with hindsight. What I am certain of is that parallels with the great *Express–Record* rivalry in the 1960s are only partly pertinent. For a start, as we have seen, the combined circulation of these two papers was well over a million. The combined circulation of the *Record* and the *Scottish Sun*, though both are very downmarket compared to the *Record* and the *Express* of the 1960s, is around 800,000.

' '

It was Kelvin Mackenzie, the legendary editor of the *Sun* in the 1980s, who hired Jack Irvine to launch the *Scottish Sun*. Irvine recalls: 'There was a rumour in the industry that Murdoch was going to launch the *Sun* in Scotland, and everybody believed that I would be offered the job. There were all sorts of mutterings by senior people at the *Record*. I came in on the morning I got the job, and I gave my resignation to the editor. He was very polite and understanding. Then I came in that night, and he attempted to punch me and had to be led away. Kelvin Mackenzie just said to me: "I want you to destroy the *Record*. I want you to sell lots of papers. Just go out and hire the guys you want and the gals you want and get stuck in." And that was my brief.'

Irvine reflects on his time as a production executive on the *Record* during the Robert Maxwell era: 'One of the ironies about Maxwell is that, if you look back, the paper was more successful under Maxwell than it is now. You'll hear a lot of old *Record* hands jokingly saying: "I wish Maxwell was back with us". If you look at the product in the Maxwell years, it was as good as it had ever been.'

Steve Sampson, who was Jack Irvine's news editor when he launched the *Scottish Sun*, is now a director of Trinity Mirror, the *Record*'s owners. He reckons that Bruce Waddell, the current *Record* editor, who was hired from the *Sun* in 2004, is the best journalist in Scotland. 'He worked for me at the *Sun*. We had to go and nick him and pay him a fortune to come over. He's head and shoulders the best editor in the country.'

Colin McLatchie is News International's, and therefore Rupert Murdoch's, senior manager in Scotland, the executive in overall charge of the Scottish editions of the *Sun*, the *News of the World*, the *Times* and the *Sunday Times*. He moved from the *Record* to News International in 1995. Colin says: 'I'd been part of the team that got the *Record* to its peak in the early 1990s. I moved for a variety of reasons. In those days, the *Record* was doing in the region of 750,000 copies a day. The gap was huge. The challenge was to continue to erode that gap. If you fast-forward to where we are now, the gap has all but disappeared. The great target we have had is to overtake the *Record*. We had that as a target for ten years, and we are now very, very close to achieving it.'

He adds: 'We have cut the *Sun*'s price aggressively, but there's no point at all in just cutting the cover price and leaving it at that. We have still got to give what the reader really wants to buy. The *Record* still has much greater resources in terms of all its many Scottish journalists. But what we can do is this. We can take the best of the UK stories, the very best of the *Sun* journalism from London, and interweave it in with the Scottish material. It's as simple as that.'

My personal view is that Bruce Waddell has, in almost impossible circumstances of constant cost-cutting, improved the *Record* editorially. But most tabloid wars are bewildering and not particularly edifying. They are not always won, obviously enough, on the simple basis of editorial quality. And there is an additional intensity about the *Record–Sun* battle because so many of the key personnel involved have switched papers. They have moved backwards and forwards, and the two titles are not as different as the *Express* and the *Record* were in the glory years of their fabulous, frenetic rivalry. In those years, the *Record* lost to the *Express*. Now it looks as if it may lose a second time.

Of one thing I am certain: whatever merit the *Scottish Sun* may have, it is not, and never will be, in the same league as the *Scottish Daily Express* in the years of its grandeur. Scottish journalism had never seen anything like that before, and I doubt if it ever will again.

5

A Paean to Pirie

One of the great demarcations in the post-war British press was between broadsheet and tabloid. The divide was never such an issue in Scotland, because for many years Scottish daily journalism had only one significant tabloid – the *Daily Record*. For me, the journalist who exemplified the *Record* at its best was John Pirie. A Dundonian, John left school at 14 and went to work in the Dundee office of the *Scottish Daily Express*. This was in 1938. Two years later, he lied about his age and joined the Royal Navy. He saw service on the Russian convoys, and later in the Mediterranean. He was on board HMS *Edinburgh* when a U-boat sank her in 1942. At the time, she was carrying £45 million in gold bullion, and John would later quip that it was an early warning that people should never trust him with their money. He survived and ended up in a camp for Allied seamen in the vicinity of Murmansk. John, always a man of strong left-wing views, was one of the British sailors who defied their officers when they were ordered not to fraternise with the Bolsheviks.

After the war, John worked for various news agencies in western Scotland and the north of England. Then he joined the *News Chronicle* in Manchester, though he was to undertake several extended stints at the paper's head office in London. He reckoned that the *Chronicle*, with its liberal values and its consistent left-of-centre slant, was the ideal paper for him. He became deputy news editor and felt he was being 'groomed for stardom'.

Then came 'Black Monday' – 17 October 1960, when at 5:30pm the *Chronicle*'s entire editorial staff were summoned to emergency meetings and informed that the edition of the paper which they were preparing would be the last one. It was a brutal end to the life of a fine newspaper that was then selling more than 1,200,000 copies a day. At the meetings, the journalists were informed that their paper was going to 'merge' with the right-wing *Daily Mail*. Some merger: all 3,500 staff on the *Chronicle* and its sister evening paper, the *Star*, lost their jobs. John later told me that what happened that night was more traumatic for him than anything he had experienced in his eventful war.

John reluctantly returned to Scotland and joined the *Daily Record*. Five years later, in 1965, he was appointed the *Record*'s education correspondent, a role he undertook with aplomb for twenty-one years until his retirement in 1986, when he joined the Scottish Examination Board in an advisory capacity.

When I was appointed education correspondent of the *Scotsman* at the end of 1973, I rapidly became aware of John's considerable reputation. That was a time of turmoil in Scottish schools. The two dominant issues were the phasing-out of corporal punishment and the raising of the school-leaving age. Emotionally and intellectually, John was utterly committed to both developments, but he was respected because he always reported fairly the views and speeches of the many teachers and parents who opposed the changes. (It may seem strange now, more than thirty years on, but the Scottish teaching profession was bitterly divided by both moves – and many teachers, including union activists, aggressively resisted them.)

A Paean to Pirie

My first few encounters with John were not propitious. He struck me as somewhat aloof and even arrogant. I remember rushing round North Lanarkshire one day early in 1974. The Scottish Under Secretary for Education, Hector Monro, was visiting various secondary schools with problematic reputations. I was following him around in a *Scotsman* pool car, a beaten-up old Ford Escort (a hand-me-down from the circulation reps) which I was driving myself, whereas John was travelling around in a limo with a driver. When I finally caught up with John at the press conference at the end of the day, a shambolic affair held in the dining hall of the final school we visited, I made some jocular remarks about our two papers. I contrasted the ways in which the *Record* and the *Scotsman* treated their journalists. John did not respond as I expected to this banter. He gave me a lecture.

First, the *Record* was a paper that understood how to treat its staff in style. Too many broadsheets, for all their airs and graces, didn't attend to that most basic of duties. (And he was right: the *Scotsman*'s staff were disgracefully underpaid.) Secondly, I should bear in mind (John's favourite phrase) that the *Record* reached far more parents, pupils and teachers than the *Scotsman* and the *Glasgow Herald* combined. I replied to this by saying that at least the *Scotsman* had sent me to this assignment in Lanarkshire; the *Herald* was nowhere to be seen. We adjourned to a pub in Airdrie and continued the conversation, stopping only for half an hour or so to phone over our copy. I was becoming quite envious of John, who could drink as much as he wanted (and he was a prodigious drinker), given that his driver was waiting patiently outside. But that conversation marked the beginning of our friendship.

Shortly afterwards, the prime minister, Ted Heath, called a snap general election on the spurious issue of who ran the country – the government or the miners. And, although the Tories gained more votes, they had fewer seats than Labour.

So, Harold Wilson returned to Downing Street, and Willie Ross returned to St Andrew's House to resume his career as Secretary of State for Scotland, and John was delighted – for about five minutes. John was honest enough to confess to me, only a week or so into the new administration, that he was disappointed and angry. He could see much trouble ahead. He was right: Ross, himself a former teacher, was in no mood to conciliate Scotland's increasingly militant teachers.

In the summer of 1974, there was a major upheaval at Scotland's leading teaching union, the Educational Institute of Scotland (EIS), when John Pollock, a charismatic head teacher from Ayrshire, who at one time had been regarded as Ross's protégé, replaced the scholarly Gilbert Bryden as the union's general secretary. Bryden was an aloof man whose apparent disdain for his own members was surpassed only by his disdain for the press. Pollock, on the other hand, made it clear from the start that he would be media-friendly. Pollock's appointment was a godsend for John Pirie; he was a man after his own heart, a combative and constantly available leader who regarded the EIS as a union, militant if need be, rather than a restrained professional institute.

Late in 1974, and on into 1975, John Pirie gave full journalistic backing in the *Record* to Pollock and his associate Fred Forrester as they orchestrated a series of increasingly bitter teachers' strikes over pay and conditions. This was both brave and controversial; many *Record* readers, while accepting that Scottish teachers were badly underpaid, were working parents. For them, the strikes were particularly disruptive. But John continued to back the teachers, and I think he played a crucial role in tempering parental anger across Scotland.

I was getting a constant stream of front-page stories in the *Scotsman* at this time, and John rarely made the front of the *Record*; but he assured me, and I believed him, that his stories were every bit as influential as mine, perhaps more so. Although the Houghton settlement that eventually ended the protracted dispute was generous, there were to be more waves of angry industrial action in Scottish schools over the next decade. John covered them all, always seeking out the human angle in his stories.

John Pollock had an intuitive understanding of John Pirie's ability to get through to a wide educational constituency, and an even wider audience of parents, via the high-selling *Record*. I was fascinated to watch how John worked during the 1974–5 dispute. He would always try to personalise each development, to give it human interest, even if it was about some arcane negotiating point. And he undoubtedly did fuse news and comment in a way that I had been taught was wrong. In a way, he was a throwback to an earlier era when there was less emphasis on objectivity in reporting. Yet his copy always had integrity, and John was regarded with both affection and respect by many whose views were very different from his. He was to receive an honorary degree from the Open University and an honorary fellowship from the EIS. The newly installed Labour government was, however, not impressed with his efforts; it complacently regarded the *Record* almost as its in-house newsletter, but nobody seemed to have told John Pirie. Fortunately, John and his supportive editor, Bernie Vickers, were not in the least put out by the hostility that was sometimes shown to John by senior Labour figures, including Willie Ross himself.

Matters improved greatly when Harold Wilson stood down and the new prime minister, Jim Callaghan, wasted no time in firing Willie Ross. The new Secretary of State for Scotland, Bruce Millan, was a Dundonian, a far less combative figure than Ross, and a man whom John Pirie already knew and liked. Not even John's role as a founding member of the breakaway Scottish Labour Party could diminish their mutual trust. Furthermore, the new Scottish Under Secretary for Education was a man with whom John struck up an immediate and very warm friendship. This man, Frank McElhone, was one of the few genuine characters of recent decades' Scottish politics. He had been a greengrocer in the Gorbals and was full of patter, but he had a shrewd political mind. He grasped the potential of John's influence, and he was soon inviting John to his room on the top floor of New St Andrew's House in the St James Centre in Edinburgh for chats about educational policy. I was invited along too – but I understood that, although I got on very well with Frank at a personal level, he was more interested in the *Record*'s readership than the *Scotsman*'s.

This was at a time when the *Scotsman* was obsessed with devolution, to which the Callaghan government was wholly committed; but Frank thought that the drive for devolution was getting in the way of the day-to-day running of Scottish affairs. I was surprised to hear the utter candour with which this man, a Minister of the Crown, albeit a junior one, spoke to us. He often sought our advice on policy matters and told us that his official advisers were unimaginative and occasionally obstructive. Sometimes he'd say, in complete seriousness: 'I could do with a good initiative this week, and so what can you gentlemen recommend?' Word of these conversations filtered through to Frank's leading civil servants and to HM Senior Inspectorate of Schools in Scotland, who were technically his educational advisers. They were not pleased. But John took his role as unofficial (and unpaid) adviser to McElhone very seriously, and constantly told him, for example, to visit a few List D schools – and then abolish them.

Frank eventually decided he'd visit a couple of the schools, and he did so in a semi-public manner, accompanied by a few pressmen. Never a man to mince his words, he was so disturbed by what he found at one school that he told us, unfortunately off the record: 'Sodom and Gomorrah had nothing on this place'. To which our colleague Iain Thorburn of the *Times Educational Supplement Scotland* responded: 'Well, Frank, we all know about Sodom, but can you please tell us what exactly went on at Gomorrah?'

Perhaps it was not too surprising that Frank McElhone did not get on with his civil servants. An exception was his press officer, Quentin Jardine, who in later life became a very successful thriller-writer. Although himself a Tory, Jardine reckoned that McElhone was a breath of fresh air, and he went out of his way to accommodate McElhone's unusual approach to his ministerial work.

＂

I learned a great deal from John Pirie. He frequently told me that any fool could write any story in 1,000 words; it took craft and skill and talent to write it in 100. A very dapper man, he told me he thought I was too scruffy. He strongly believed that the 'gentlemen' of the press had to keep up appearances. (Indeed, when we were attending educational conferences together, it was often assumed by people who didn't know us that John was representing the *Scotsman* and I was representing the *Record*.) He also told me I was too concerned with official reports, inquiries and so on. I was always determined to get leaks on these; John said they didn't matter to the people in the streets. Human interest, he always insisted – that was what counted. Although we often found ourselves covering the same story from different angles, we also nursed a rivalry. Early on in our friendship, he told me that most press conferences were a waste of time. What you should do, he said, is wait until they are finished, hover around the platform party, and try for a few words from the key players in private. You'll often get the real story that way.

Shortly afterwards, slightly to my regret, I used this tactic to get one over on him. We were both in Aberdeen to cover a special meeting of Aberdeen Education Committee, which had been convened to suspend – in effect dismiss – the man who was then Scotland's most controversial head teacher, the great radical educationist R. F. Mackenzie. After a very highly charged, angry and emotive debate, the decision to suspend Mackenzie was taken by ten votes to six. John was looking for a phone to file his copy before catching the train back to Glasgow; I managed to grab a word with Mackenzie, who was being ushered out of the Aberdeen Corporation chambers by his family. He was in a highly emotional state. He said he could not possibly speak then, but he'd be happy to see me at his farmhouse by the River Dee later that evening.

I changed my plans to return to Edinburgh and decided to stay overnight in Aberdeen. Later, at Mackenzie's house, we talked long into the night, and he gave me an exceptional interview that amounted to a devastating critique not just of Scottish education but of Scotland itself. It appeared in the *Scotsman* twenty-four hours later as an extended news feature called 'The Unbowed Head'. John Pirie phoned me up, pretending to be furious. He was coming through to Edinburgh. To sort me out. I was quite worried. But then he added: 'And I've got a bottle of malt for you. Well done. You cleaned up.'

In a postscript to that anecdote, I should record John's intro to his story in the *Daily Record* on the morning after the Mackenzie suspension. It simply read: 'I accuse Aberdeen Education Committee of treachery'.

❝❞

In the summer of 1977, I was especially grateful for John's friendship and support. I had acquired a precious ticket for the England–Scotland football international at Wembley. Unfortunately, the game was being played on the final day of the EIS annual meeting, which was being held at Stirling University. I told the *Scotsman* news desk of my problem; but, although I had already worked several six-day weeks and one or two seven-day weeks that year – it was a period of constant controversy and news in Scottish education – they insisted that I should cover the EIS meeting.

They pointed out that I was the specialist, and the *Scotsman's* readership would expect me to cover the whole conference. There was some sense in this; at that time, thanks mainly to Pollock and Forrester, EIS conferences were consistently newsworthy and full of incident. But I was determined to get to Wembley. I think that, had I gone to Eric Mackay, my editor, he would have overruled the news editor, Stuart Brown, and his deputy; but that would have vitiated my future relations with the men I had to work for day in, day out. So, I decided to take a risk.

I flew down to London on the Saturday morning (with Dennis Canavan, the Labour MP and former teacher, who had been attending the EIS meeting as an observer), met up with my pals and saw the game, which Scotland won 2–1, and then we celebrated all night. I had made an arrangement that I'd phone John Pirie on the Sunday morning. I had been told that I was expected to supply a page lead and probably two other stories for Monday's *Scotsman*. John very kindly offered to phone in three stories direct to the *Scotsman* copytakers, but I thought that this would be too chancy. Instead, I asked him to give me an account of the main events of the final day of the conference. I would then phone the stories over from a callbox as we progressed north (I was getting a lift back to Edinburgh).

John chose rather to phone over three complete stories to me, impeccably written in the best *Scotsman* style. I didn't need to change a word. I think he was giving me a subtle lesson: he could have worked for the *Scotsman* with ease; I'd have found it more difficult to work for the *Record*. Anyway, everything worked out fine. My only problem connected with that weekend of deceit was that, two days later, the *Scotsman* news desk asked me to investigate stories that Dennis Canavan, who of course had been in our party, was one of those who had invaded the pitch and dug up the Wembley turf at the end of the game. My investigations were not assiduous.

❛ ❜

John Pirie had left school as soon as he could to work in a newspaper office, and he was suspicious of the trend for university to become the preferred route to journalism. He had been attracted by the excitement of a newspaper career, but he often told me that newspapers were losing their character because they were being produced by people who hadn't served a proper apprenticeship.

John had knocked around a bit, and he had a good understanding of people and of how the world worked. He was a natural gentleman, a courteous and civil colleague. He was a serious drinker who was also a good family man. He was an autodidact with a much wider general knowledge than most of today's graduates; he was known in press circles as 'the professor'. Progressive in outlook and politically committed, he was also fair and open-minded. (Surprisingly, he struck up a friendship with Max Beloff, the founder of Britain's first independent university, and a supporter of Margaret Thatcher.)

John Pirie died in October 2005. He was a fine exemplar of a special type of Scottish journalist: self-made, self-taught, highly literate, a keen questioner and a good listener, and a man who had an innate, instinctive understanding of his readership – a type that is disappearing all too fast.

6

Hot Metal and Acts of Disunion

For many Scottish journalists who started their careers in the 1950s, 1960s or 1970s, the short journey from the editorial floor down to the caseroom or printing shop was not exactly a journey to hell. But it was a journey from a relatively safe and comfortable environment, where they were in control, to a nether world of mayhem, dirt, din and confusion where they were, if not downright irrelevant, very much second-class citizens. Newspaper production in the days of hot metal may have been noisy, filthy and altogether Dickensian – but, my goodness, it was exciting.

The veteran journalist Bob Jeffrey, who worked on the production of five different Glasgow papers, recalls: 'The pages were made up in these huge metal formes. The Linotype operators produced the slugs, little lines of metal the width of a column. These were put together on this metal frame on a slab of steel that was called the stone. And of course the caseroom was where all your mistakes would catch up with you. The pages were drawn upstairs, on the editorial floor, but it was downstairs that they were converted into metal and put together on the stone. If the stories did not fit exactly – unlike nowadays, where you can change them instantly on your screen – then the printer had either to cut some metal out or squeeze it all in. You could save half an inch by simply getting the upmaker to tighten the metal up. And the clock's ticking all the time, and the pages are phased to go down to the machine room in their proper sequence, and if your page is holding the whole caboodle up, then you're in big trouble. There was a lot of pressure in that. Illustrations were made with metal plates, so that if you miscalculated the size of a picture the upmaker had to take it out of the page frame, take it off its mount and then saw it down to the right size with his saw. So, journalists who consistently got the size of the illustrations wrong were very unpopular with the printers.'

The sheer shock of the first visit to the caseroom is well described by Julie Davidson, recalling her days at the *Press and Journal*'s old headquarters in Broad Street, Aberdeen. 'I definitely felt that this was my initiation into the *real* world of newspapers. You entered the Linotype room, and it was a very macho environment. There were about thirty men, and you were the only woman, a young woman, walking in. But there was no lechery. The men were gruff, but polite and helpful. There was a complete lack of natural light. The printers were all grey-faced men wearing grey overalls. The hot metal itself was grey, and it was cast in huge grey Linotype machines. So, the caseroom was a sort of demented, clattering pit of a place, a world that was monochromatic. Indeed, what I remember most is this total absence of colour, and of course the noise, the constant noise – you had to shout to make yourself heard above the Linotype machines. Some of the printers could lip-read. And, as your page was being "made up" on the stone, you'd realise that your writing, your page, was utterly dependent on the dexterity and skill of this man, the upmaker, working against the clock to get the page away on time. It was certainly exciting, and it would have been even more exciting if I had realised at the time that I was living through the last ten minutes in the long, long hegemony of hot metal.'

Murray Ritchie has similar memories of his first visit to the *Glasgow Herald*'s old caseroom in Mitchell Street, Glasgow. 'The first time I went down there, I actually bumped into this printer. He was like a head waiter with this tray of burning hot metal in his hand, and I hit him. And I don't know how he did it, but he managed to catch this shower of metal, and we didn't lose a slug. After that, I was terrified to go into the caseroom. The printers wouldn't let you touch type. It was absolutely forbidden under the very strict demarcation rules that existed then. You could poke the type with the end of your pencil if you had something you particularly wanted to point out. We had quite a prickly relationship with the printers, but in times of stress they were usually on our side.'

Some of the journalists who were best at working with printers in the caseroom had previously been printers themselves. A fine example was Willie Kemp, the legendary sports editor of the *Scotsman* in the 1960s and 1970s. When I was learning – and I was not a very good pupil – about production journalism under Willie's tutelage, he sent me down to the *Scotsman* caseroom for the first time with a mischievous twinkle in his eye. I found myself in this huge room – more like a factory floor – with the rows of incredibly noisy Linotype machines, clanking away. They were massive, almost human machines, with long mechanical arms moving up and down in this strange demented rhythm.

It took me some time to find the sports stone, and I felt that Willie had thrown me to the wolves. Luckily, I had a helpful upmaker – most of them were pretty decent, unless you touched the type – and the sports pages, competently and accurately drawn by Willie, required only a few small cuts. (The easiest way to cut was to ask the upmaker simply to take off the last paragraph, or paragraphs, of a story, but this practice was rightly frowned upon as being expedient rather than editorially responsible.) Surplus type was tossed by the upmaker into big metal bins beside each stone; and this added to the din, and to the worry – because the metal, once in the bin, was lost forever.

In some ways, the *Scotsman* machine room, even lower down at the very bottom of the venerable old building, on Market Street under North Bridge, Edinburgh, was the most thrilling place to be. This was especially the case when the button was pressed and the vast printing machines whirred. And then they roared into action, and the whole building began to vibrate, and the first pristine editions of that night's paper would appear on these peculiar, long, rackety, meandering conveyor belts that carried the fruits of our labours from the roaring machines to the waiting vans. Yet that excitement was too obvious. The caseroom was where the paper was really put together, and the men – they were all men – who worked in this extraordinary environment among their flongs, quoins, mangles, tweezers, sticks, stones, slugs, galley proofs and Linotype machines were the real heroes of newspaper production in the messy, glorious, inefficient, thrilling, bad old days of hot metal, before the new computerised printing technology changed everything.

These printers were highly skilled – more so than most journalists – and they could work with extraordinary precision under extreme pressure. Yet they have suffered, ironically enough, a bad press. The wider public associate past newspaper militancy with print workers, not journalists. This is in part because of the great Wapping set-piece dispute in London in 1985–6, when Rupert Murdoch and Charles Wilson took on the printing unions in the last great industrial battle of the Thatcher years. But, in Scotland, it was the journalists rather than the printers who tended to be more militant. Most of the stoppages in Scottish newspapers that I can recall between 1970 and 1990 were caused by journalists. The most notorious, the greatest own goal in

Scottish newspaper history, was the dispute that in effect terminated the *Scottish Daily Express* in 1974.

In some ways, Beaverbrook himself was indirectly responsible, because he was so keen for his Express Group to be the biggest and the richest and the most powerful group that he simply threw money at all problems. This resulted in an unrealistic and over-generous culture that pervaded every aspect of newspaper production – from journalists' expenses to gross overmanning in the machine room.

Jack Webster recalls: 'In the good days, the balmy days, the *Express* had built up its staff. The *Express* had always had two or three people where other papers had one, so the *Express* was overstaffed. Then the time came when they wanted to pull the belt in a wee bit. By this time, a lot of young journalists were coming into the *Express*. They were much more interested in politics than in journalism. These journalists dug their heels in. It was journalists, not printers, who brought about the downfall of the *Scottish Daily Express*. The leader of the union power on the *Express* was a journalist called Denny McGhee, and Denny was your typical Glasgow man. He was at the kind of tail end of the old Glasgow comedian era, and when he came back from the war – and he'd had quite a war – he was a feed for Lex McLean at the Pavilion in Renfield Street. He used to tell us great tales about that. Then he found his way into journalism. He lay fairly quiet on the *Express* for a few years, and then gradually his political side came out and he emerged as the union leader. Then the later group of young left-wingers clustered around him and in the end overtook him. But he had tremendous power, as typified by what happened one night when he objected to a cartoon that had come up from London, a cartoon by the famous Cummings. It was something to do with Denny's Catholicism, I think – this was a cartoon about the IRA to which he personally took exception – and that night this one man managed to stop the paper getting out.

115

That was the kind of power he had. Well, in the last year of the *SDE*, from March 1973 to March 1974, we lost sixteen days of no publication at all, and fifty-six further nights of one edition only. Newspapers are the most perishable of all commodities. You just cannot do that.'

On St Patrick's Day 1974, the Beaverbrook management (Beaverbrook himself had died ten years earlier) finally decided to cut their losses and shut down the printing presses in Albion Street, Glasgow, and move to Manchester. Nearly 2,000 jobs were lost. Many of the best journalists in Scotland found themselves on the streets. It was a devastating, unparalleled blow for the Scottish newspaper industry.

And yet journalists elsewhere did not heed the lessons. For example, through the 1980s, there were three serious journalists' disputes on the *Scotsman*. The *Scotsman's* circulation had been steadily built up during the 1970s; all this effort was frittered away in the following decade. The first of the disputes, in 1981, was beginning just as I left the *Scotsman* to join the *Sunday Standard* in Glasgow. I was excited by my new job on a brand new paper, but I kept in touch with my former colleagues in the east, and I heard many sad stories about the divisions and stresses of an intensive industrial dispute. (This particular one lasted just over a fortnight.)

There was no doubt that the *Scotsman* staff had been disgracefully underpaid. But, like most newspaper disputes in those days, the eventual settlement was essentially fudged. It solved nothing in the long term. There were to be two more debilitating journalists' strikes at the *Scotsman* before the decade was out, including a particularly acrimonious one in 1987.

❝❞

Hot Metal and Acts of Disunion

By the mid-1980s, I had become deputy editor of the *Glasgow Herald*, and I was sometimes involved in 'negotiations' between the management and the journalists. I use the inverted commas because, if the truth be told, these meetings tended to be ritual war dances at which little was achieved other than the spouting of overblown rhetoric (on both sides). The real negotiations were often undertaken informally and quickly, too quickly, off site.

In 1985, a minor but long-standing journalists' dispute on the *Herald* suddenly escalated. The journalists held a protracted meeting that, if it had continued into the night, would have stopped production. This was a well-tried tactic; management, fearful of losing all the revenue that disappeared with the loss of one night's paper, often backed down at the last minute. But, on this particular evening, Terry Cassidy, the abrasive managing director of the Herald Group, was in no mood to back down. Arnold Kemp, the *Herald*'s editor, was abroad, and so I was the most senior executive journalist around. But I was not too worried, because Harry Conroy was in the building. Harry had made his name as both a business and a property specialist with the *Daily Record* and also as a fiery union orator. But he was always a pragmatic and responsible journalists' leader.

The *Record* management often gave him leave of absence to try to resolve journalists' problems on other papers. This was very generous of the *Record*, and perhaps not sufficiently appreciated by the other houses whch benefited from Harry's mediation, though some of Harry's more cynical colleagues reckoned that it was simply a means of getting him well away from the *Record* offices at Anderston Quay. Harry noted later that his union career had taken him into many papers and involved him in many industrial disputes, but he believed that most of his interventions had led to solutions. He believed that he was very rarely involved in stopping the presses – and I would endorse that.

In the summer of 1985, Harry was elected UK general secretary of the National Union of Journalists, and he was due to move to London when the dispute flared at the *Herald*. As the mandatory meeting on the editorial floor dragged on and on, I began to worry about that night's paper. I consulted Harry, and he assured me that it was just the usual brinkmanship and that the journalists would return to work in time to produce the paper. But they didn't; for once, Harry had not read the situation correctly.

At about 11:30pm, Terry Cassidy called me up to his office and said he'd managed to reach a deal with the print unions (who usually backed the journalists in their disputes, and vice versa). Terry said the basis of his deal was that if the most senior editorial executive in the building – me – were to appear in the caseroom even if only for ten minutes or so, the printers would produce a paper. I thought this was absurd. There would be no editorial copy in the 'paper'; it would consist only of ads and ad features, thrown together in a messy way. The 'paper' might save a little revenue, but it would be a laughing stock. So, I declined.

With quiet menace, Terry – and, my goodness, he could be menacing – told me that this was not a request, it was an instruction. To buy time, I asked for a few minutes to think about it. I got hold of Harry Conroy and asked if there was any chance, at this desperately late stage, of a return to work. Harry understood my predicament, but said he was afraid not. I knew I could make only one decision. The *'Herald'* that would be produced would be a dog's breakfast, and I'd lose all credibility with my striking colleagues. So, I told Terry no, though I feared for my job. No *Herald* appeared, and a lot of revenue was lost. Terry was spitting blood.

Twenty-four hours later, mainly thanks to the good offices of Harry Conroy, the dispute was settled, and Terry called me back to his big office, high above the famous Ramshorn Kirk graveyard on the other side of the building from Albion Street. I remember looking down at the Ramshorn far below and wondering if this was to be a graveyard moment for me. But Terry simply said that, as far as he and I were concerned, the events of the previous forty-eight hours had not taken place, and the slate was clean. I thought that was a big, magnanimous gesture from a very tough but very decent managing director.

Soon, Harry Conroy was to be involved in an infinitely bigger dispute, the extended showdown at Wapping. But there was never to be another serious dispute on the *Herald*. Partly, this marked the post-Wapping realism; partly it marked the spirit that Liam Kane engendered after his management buy-out of the Herald Group from Lonrho in 1992. In the years after the buy-out, it was well understood by all the unions at Albion Street that the future of the papers was fragile and that any serious dispute could be devastating. Liam managed to shed more than 400 jobs without a single day's lost production, which even in the post-Wapping era was a considerable achievement.

Meanwhile, the technological changes in newspaper production ensured one thing: most of the old printing skills were redundant. Journalists were of course still needed to produce newspapers (to some people's regret), but most of the printers weren't. Computerised 'single keystroke' technology altered everything. Some newspaper houses managed the consequent changes with dignity and sensitivity. On the *Herald* in the late 1980s, for example, quite a few printers were retrained as journalists.

But the old caserooms, with their never-to-be-forgotten smell of hot metal, din, organised confusion and amazing Heath Robinson contraptions that were the Linotype machines – these vanished for ever. Even the newsrooms changed: no longer did journalists write copy with battered typewriters; now there were computer keyboards and monitors and workstations. Hot-desking was suddenly the order of the day. People didn't talk to each other, or shout at each other, but sent e-mails. Editorial floors became quieter, more sanitised and insulated, but far less lively and frenetic places. And in many ways, it has to be said, newspapers declined as a result. The general public certainly thought so.

It would, however, be wrong to over-romanticise the days of hot metal. Working in the infernal, dirty, noisy, overheated environment of an old-style caseroom was certainly not good for your health. And there were far too many print unions, and all of them had the ability to stop the paper. This was a recipe for anarchy; in Fleet Street, the unions took it in turns to orchestrate disputes. One month the electricians, the next month the upmakers, the next the van-loaders, the next the platemakers, the next the craftsmen who dealt with the ink ducts. The demarcations were many and ludicrous. And the overmanning got worse, and the Spanish practices escalated, and the wages became exorbitant. This was less the case in Scotland, where, as I have indicated, the journalists tended to use industrial muscle more than the printers.

Looking back on those years, Colin McClatchie, News International's general manager in Scotland, is reluctant to place all the blame on the unions. He says: 'I suspect that in those days the proprietors were as much to blame as the unions. When one particular title was missing, everyone else hastily printed a lot more copies to take advantage, and gleefully rubbed their hands together at managing to increase their sales at someone else's expense without realising that in the long term it was absolutely destroying the industry. I suspect that, in the period leading up to Wapping, many of the seeds of the decline of the industry were being sown, in terms of discouraging regular readership.'

There is still an ongoing dispute. It is not an industrial one, rather one of historical interpretation. Former union leaders like Harry Conroy insist that the strikes at Wapping and elsewhere were not really about the introduction of new technology, which was just the occasion of the dispute. The real point of the dispute was de-unionisation. Yet Harry, always supremely realistic, admits that the print unions too often abused their power. He felt that this abuse was often not the fault of national presidents and general secretaries but of chapel officials. He also believes that the unions were beginning to reform in the mid-1980s, and he likes to remind people that the most powerful print union on Fleet Street, the National Graphical Association, had reached an agreement with the National Union of Journalists which would have allowed 'direct input' by journalists. Unfortunately, this came too late to prevent Wapping.

In retrospect, I believe that the two processes – the introduction of new technology and the loss of union power – were inextricably caught up in each other. Much of the behaviour of the newspaper unions in the 1960s and 1970s and into the 1980s was unacceptable. There was without doubt a situation of near-anarchy in many if not most of the big newspaper houses, especially in Fleet Street. And Scotland's best newspaper, the *Scottish Daily Express*, was destroyed by extreme union militancy – excessive militancy which luckily was far less prevalent in other Scottish houses. Also, I think it is important to remember how soul-destroying it could be for a journalist who had worked on a strong and perhaps really significant story, only to see it disappear forever because of what was as often as not a relatively minor, maybe even a frivolous, dispute.

The shelf life of newspapers is notoriously short; but it is infinitely better to have them in existence, even if only for the relatively few hours before they become the wrapping for chips, than for them not to exist at all. On the other hand, as Colin McClatchie candidly admits, the managements were weak and short-sighted – before Murdoch – and you could not blame the unions for exploiting this weakness. And the production of newspapers, involving so many different skills and so many different unions, rendered the industry particularly vulnerable.

Finally, as a nostalgic footnote to all this, I have to record that one of the saddest developments in the industry from a sentimental perspective is that the vast machine rooms, where the papers are actually printed, are now housed in modern plants. These are usually adjacent to motorways, and a long way from the newspaper offices where the journalists work. Journalists of my generation, working a late or a back shift, were always aware of exactly when the presses had started to run. Sometimes we could hear the warning klaxon; but even if we didn't, although we were working several floors above the machine room, we'd always sense that sudden vibration that sent a kind of tremor, a little shudder, across the editorial floor, and then we'd hear from downstairs the distant rumble of those mighty machines as they roared into action. We were rolling, we were in business.

Or not, as the case might be. Too often, for one reason or another, the great presses didn't roll.

7

Booze, Beaverbrook and the Big Bad City

This is very much an anecdotal chapter, about pubs and drinking and crime and expenses and Lord Beaverbrook and, above all, about Glasgow. Although Ian Bruce of the *Herald* had his own personal journalistic triumph in the Falklands, many thousands of miles from Glasgow, he is in no doubt that Glasgow is the essential heart of Scottish journalism. Ian says: 'I agree with the idea that if you've never worked in Glasgow then you cannot really call yourself a Scottish journalist. Glasgow is certainly the hardest school in UK journalism, and it has a magnificent journalistic heritage. I'd describe it as the Holy City of journalism.'

Fidelma Cook recalls joining the *Daily Record* from its sister paper the *Mirror* in London. 'Glasgow had this incredible reputation. When I was sent up here by the *Mirror*, I'd never been to Scotland in my life. The *Mirror* editor told me: "Fidelma, this will be the most fantastic training for you. If you can work in Glasgow, you can work anywhere in the world." Glasgow was considered the toughest newspaper case, because of the competition – and also because it was a tough city. In those days, court cases, murders, those sorts of things were the stuff of the paper, and not celebrity as you see now. It was the reverse. Imagine all the celebrity stuff you see – well, we did it with murderers and axemen and nutters.

And I would have bet any team, any *Daily Record* or *Scottish Daily Express* team, against any from Fleet Street. They'd have knocked them into a cocked hat. Which is why we were paid Fleet Street rates, to keep us there and in recognition of the fact that the papers were major national papers.'

Glasgow's gritty image – which I suspect it still quite likes – was partly based on an infamous but best-selling novel first published in 1935. *No Mean City*, about razor gangs and other thugs, was written by Alexander McArthur and then 'tidied up' by his co-author, the journalist H. Kingsley Long. The novel was presented luridly by its publishers as 'a terrible story of drink, poverty, moral corruption and brutality'. McArthur and Long, well aware of the outcry their work would provoke, craftily provided an appendix. In it, they provided references to various stories about crime and gangsterdom in the *Daily Record*, the *Evening Times* and the *Sunday Mail* – though not the *Glasgow Herald* – to give their work of fiction some semblance of documentary authority.

Growing up in Aberdeen in the 1950s, I was well aware that Glasgow – where I had been born – was commonly regarded as a city of danger and degradation. Some folk in Aberdeen genuinely believed that, if they were foolhardy enough to venture to Glasgow, they would at best be assailed by violent drunks, at worst knifed by thugs or shot by gangsters. Glasgow was the big bad city.

Then, in the summer of 1958, came an event that was an utter godsend to such people. Covered by the entire Scottish press, and by the huge-selling *Scottish Daily Express* with a kind of excessively fascinated intensity, the trial of Peter Manuel, a 32-year-old psychopath, served to confirm all the prejudices that were current about Glasgow. In some respects, Manuel was a fairly typical petty Glasgow criminal. But he was also a mass murderer. In 1956 and 1957, he had committed a series of nasty killings, not on the mean streets of Glasgow itself, but in the douce territory of bungalows and villas (he specialised in breaking into such homes) in the area immediately to the south and east of the city, a triangle bounded by Mount Vernon to the north, High Burnside to the south and Uddingston to the east. Manuel himself lived on the fringes of this territory, in a council house in Birkenshaw, just to the north of Uddingston.

The fourteen-day trial was extraordinarily dramatic. Midway through it, Manuel dismissed his distinguished counsel and conducted his own defence, with considerable forensic skill. At the climax of the trial, Manuel, in the dock, questioned a Glasgow businessman in a wheelchair, each accusing the other of the same murders. But it was the incidental evidence that provided the most powerful endorsement of the idea of Glasgow as a low-life city of gangsters, hard men and pervasive crime. The daily reports of the trial were read avidly, and discussed even more avidly, throughout Scotland. Glasgow was revealed, almost uncovered, as a city where crime was regarded as a normal part of life and where guns passed from criminal to criminal in pubs with routine casualness. Here was a nether world of minor criminals who were constantly in and out of Barlinnie Prison and who carried out commissions for larger, shadowy figures. There was evidence about a huge illegal gambling 'school' on the banks of the Clyde, sometimes attended by as many as 300 punters. Manuel was convicted of eight murders, though he probably committed several others, and was sentenced to death. His life ended at Barlinnie Prison at one minute past 8am on Friday, 11 July 1958.

There was already a public appetite for stories about crime and criminals, particularly in Glasgow; but this remarkable trial created a near-frenzy. As well as reporting future trials, the newspapers – particularly the *Daily Record* and the *Scottish Daily Express*, and to a lesser extent the two Glasgow evening papers, the *Times* and the *Citizen* – got into the habit of buying up the family of the victim, the family of the assailant, or sometimes even the accused himself if he were lucky enough to receive a 'not proven' verdict. Alan Cochrane, formerly of the *Express*, recalls: 'There were all manner of scuffles on the steps of the High Court in Glasgow, between the *Record* and the *Citizen* and the *Times* and the *Express*. There were car chases all over Glasgow.'

In 1961, a man called Walter Scott Ellis was acquitted of murder on a 'not proven' verdict. The immediate consequence of the acquittal was more than a mere scuffle on the steps of the High Court; this time there was a riot. The *Scottish Daily Express* had paid serious money for Ellis's exclusive story, but that did not prevent rival papers, some of which also understood that they had done deals, from trying to get hold of him. David Scott, who was then with the *Express*, remembers: 'Reporters from various different newspapers thought they had exclusive access to this man, and the fight sprawled onto the street outside the court. There must have been about forty or fifty people involved.'

❛ ❜

Glasgow remains a complex, teeming city, and it would be disgraceful to present it as merely a sort of Keystone Kops circus for criminals and the pressmen chasing them. It remains Scotland's media capital, despite the arrival of the Scottish Parliament in Edinburgh. Both BBC Scotland and Scottish Television are moving to new headquarters on the south side of the Clyde; but the significant point is that they are staying in Glasgow, not moving east. And, of course, Glasgow produces far more newspapers than Edinburgh does.

The eminent music critic Conrad Wilson started his working life in the Netherlands, then worked as a journalist in London and, for many years, Edinburgh, before he finally moved through to the *Glasgow Herald*. He says: 'I had found that I was not being allowed to write controversially for the *Scotsman* any more. One *Scotsman* editor actually ordered me not to review Scottish Opera because I was being too critical – yes, a critic being too critical! He announced his decision on the front page, saying that Scottish Opera and I needed a rest from each other ... so I reckoned the *Scotsman* had lost its nerve. Eventually, in 1991, I moved to Glasgow. I felt the *Scotsman* had detached itself from everything that mattered. And I soon felt that, by moving to Glasgow, I'd been set free. I found it enormously exciting and stimulating to be working in this city where everything seemed to be happening, certainly in the media and in the arts. I was energised and reinvigorated by the move to Glasgow, I'm absolutely certain of that.'

Glasgow will always be a city apart. Another writer who wrote gently and perceptively about Glasgow was G. S. Fraser, who reckoned that, if there was a kind of horror about Glasgow, there was also a kind of cosiness. Fraser understood that Glasgow had little thought for the rest of Scotland – and, as for the rest of Scotland, Glasgow was strangely alien to it.

Another eminent literary man, the poet Hugh MacDiarmid, wrote about what he called the dour drinkers of Glasgow, and characterised Glasgow pubs as being for connoisseurs of the morose. In my experience, that is palpable nonsense, certainly as far as the various Glasgow bars frequented by journalists are concerned. These clamorous places were always the scene of ongoing exchanges – of information, tips, trade-offs and goods (I have seen a man trying hard to sell a monkey in a Glasgow bar) as well as the fluent exchange of banter and backchat. The best of these pubs, in my biased opion, was the Press Bar in Albion Street (also known as Tom's Bar), run by the legendary McEntee family. The Press Bar was literally part of the building in which the *Scottish Daily Express* was produced. In those days, it was the Express Bar. (Later, when the *Herald* moved into the *Express* building, the 'EX' was lopped off the sign with neat Glasgow pragmatism.)

Ian Bruce says: 'For so many *Express* and *Citizen* journalists and later *Herald* and *Evening Times* journalists, the Press Bar was not just their pub, it was their office too. It was also a bank. It had the advantage over most banks that it didn't charge interest and sold good beer. Once, a long time ago, I had to get to Northern Ireland in a great hurry. The float on the *Herald* news desk had no cash, just IOUs. So, I went down to the Press Bar and they gave me £250 out of the till, just like that.'

Murray Ritchie says: 'The level of drinking came as shock to some visitors to British journalism. I remember the *Baltimore Sun* sent over to the *Herald*, on an English-Speaking Union exchange, a husband-and-wife reporting team. On their first night, Ian Bruce took them down to the Press Bar, which was heaving. This woman from Baltimore was shocked by the sight of all these journalists quaffing away. She said: "You know we'd be sacked in the US if we behaved like this, it's simply not allowed. What does your editor say?" And Ian Bruce said: "I don't know, why don't you ask him?" And there was Arnold Kemp three feet away, swallowing large gins with his staff.'

When he was finally able to give up teaching and become a full-time journalist, Jack McLean developed a routine that was part-bravado, part-celebration of his liberation. On the day he had to produce his weekly column, he would drink all day. He averred, with some justification, that imbibing a long succession of sharpeners ensured lively copy. He preferred to drink at Heraghty's on the south side of town. Sometimes, when he turned up at about 5pm to get down to work, some mischievous elements in the *Herald* would entice him down to the Press Bar, where he would have one or three top-ups. If this happened, Jack tended to require a wee nap before he got on with his writing.

So, he'd go up to the editorial floor and try to find a discreet place for his little snooze. On one particular night, he spotted the antique oak desk of the business editor, who was away. The desk had a wonderful, capacious kneehole. Jack crawled in and promptly fell asleep. About an hour later, a panic was under way. Jack's copy had not been produced. People were vaguely aware that he was somewhere in the building, but could not find him.

A somewhat sheepish search party reported to the editor that he had simply disappeared. Arnold Kemp said, in all seriousness, that he'd sniff Jack out. And so he marched across the newsroom, nostrils flaring, and sure enough he quickly found Jack snuggled up in the kneehole. But Jack was so soundly asleep that nobody could wake him, though he was being prodded and shaken and even kicked. So, once again, Arnold proved himself to be an editor of resource. He walked back to his office, produced a bottle of whisky, returned to the sleeping columnist, opened the bottle and held it right under his nose. Jack awoke with a start and gave his head a terrible bash on the desk. But he was alive, he was awake, and he went on to write a superb column.

As for the *Daily Record*, it had not one but two pubs down by the river at Anderston Quay, the CopyCat and the Off the Record. I preferred the CopyCat and sometimes drank there with John Pirie, though I felt it lacked the chancy, edgy character of the Press Bar. But I believe that the best story about drinking and journalists in Glasgow is *Record*-based, and it comes from Fidelma Cook. 'The *Record* were the first paper up here to introduce a doctor and a nurse on site. Unfortunately, the first week the doctor was there, one reporter went down to get his check. He'd been out the night before, and the doctor leaned across to him and said: "Are you drinking?" And the reporter said: "Yeah". And the doctor said: "What?" And the reporter said: "Oh, anything, whatever you've got, I'm quite happy".'

❝❞

It would be wrong to suggest that the link between drinking and journalism was confined to Glasgow, or that the drinking was wholly devoid of professional purpose. Bars frequented by journalists tended to attract people with information or tips, or what I used to call shallow background. Much of this, but by no means all of it, was rubbish; even so, many useful contacts were formed in the pub. Among the Press Bar's more reputable clientele were policemen and lawyers, including several quite high-powered figures. There were also academics from Strathclyde University, minor criminals, musicians, councillors and many others.

In Edinburgh, the *Scotsman* and *Evening News* staff had within yards of the back (staff) door of their marvellous old building two fine pubs in Fleshmarket Close, the Jinglin' Geordie and the Halfway House. In the 1970s, I spent too much of my life in the Halfway House, which was run by a masterful publican of the old school, Alex Lannie. Alex famously once told a couple of dilettante graduate trainees from the *Scotsman*, who were slowly sipping their half-pints in an effete manner, that if they didn't drink more quickly they could get out and take their custom elsewhere.

There was a kind of informal demarcation; the two pubs had clearly understood clienteles. The Halfway House was patronised by journalists, lawyers, detectives, railway workers from Waverley Station and production staff from the *Scotsman's* caseroom and machine room. The Jinglin' Geordie, marginally more upmarket, and further up the close, was the watering hole of more pretentious journalists, city councillors, advocates and footballers. When the more savvy visiting journalists arrived at Waverley, they often made their first stop in town the Halfway House, where they'd soon get an idea of what was going on.

One thing about both these pubs was that women were always made very welcome. This was not always the case in some Scottish journalists' pubs. My wife, Julie Davidson, tells a story about Aberdeen in the 1960s. 'Two Australian girls, they were tourists, tried to get into the City Bar for a drink. They were told: "Sorry ladies, men only". And they immediately spotted Pearl Murray and her great friend Ethel Simpson, respectively the women's editor and the chief reporter of the *P&J*, sitting at a table further back in the bar. And one of the Australians said: "These women, they're drinking, why can't we get in?" And the response came: "They're nae women, lassie, they're reporters".'

❛❜

Much of this drinking was paid for on expenses. Even on the *Scotsman*, a tightly run ship if ever there was one, journalists managed to put through some unlikely expense claims. The investigative journalist George Hume used to put at the bottom of his claim each week the two words 'To mingling'. And he charged, for this 'mingling', £5 – a lot of money in those days. The *Herald*'s business editor, Ronnie Dundas, would conclude his weekly claim with the mysterious line 'To grats and cloaks', which, being translated, meant assorted gratuities and cloakroom fees.

My favourite anecdote about expenses concerns Sam White, one of Beaverbrook's most indulged correspondents, who acted as a Paris diarist for the *Evening Standard* and the *Daily Express* over many years. He was also reputed to have worked briefly for the *Scotsman*. White used to spend a great deal of time at the splendid bar of the Crillon, the very posh hotel just off the Place de la Concorde. For many years, his weekly expense claims featured the delphic item 'To flowers for Baroness X'. Eventually, even Beaverbrook's accountants had had enough, and they sent White a curt message: 'That's enough Baroness X'. The next week, White sent in an even larger claim, this time marked: 'Flowers for the funeral of Baroness X'.

Beaverbrook had a lot to answer for. His larger-than-life, somewhat rascally approach to journalism mirrored his own immoderate personality and was predicated on the belief that his papers simply had to be more exuberant, more stylish, more talked about than all the others. This meant, among many other things, that his staff would be the biggest spenders. He sometimes signed up journalists and doubled their salaries overnight. The *Express* hired planes without thinking about it; it had a network of high-spending correspondents all over the world. The *Express* staff behaved with an extravagance and style that made everyone else think it, if not the norm, at least the standard that had to be aspired to. Shortly before he died, in 1964, Beaverbrook was urged to support a 'reign of terror' by his executives against ever more exorbitant expense claims. Happily, the great man demurred.

Beaverbrook wanted his papers to reflect his persona. He adored journalists, and wanted to keep his staff – if not always his editors – happy. He was a man who ignored convention, in matters big and small. He had gargantuan appetites. He wore dark suits and brown shoes, he chased women, he guzzled maple syrup. He presided over very right-wing newspapers written by very left-wing journalists. He disliked consistency. He was unpredictable and mischievous. He never booked at any restaurant, anywhere in the world, believing correctly that a table would always be found for him. He drank whisky (Black Label), champagne, and yet more champagne. He relentlessly cultivated the few who were even richer than he was. One of his editors remarked: 'He's Allah, and the rest of us are his prophets'.

But then, as I have noted elsewhere, they don't make proprietors like Beaverbrook any more.

❛❜

People who have worked in other professions, trades, callings or crafts (journalism is not exactly any of these, but I think trade is the best word) often listen to the stories about the drinking in a slightly aghast, puzzled way. How on earth were the papers ever produced? One answer is that much, maybe most, of the drinking was done by writing journalists – the reporters, feature-writers, sportswriters, specialist correspondents, leader-writers and so on. The papers were actually produced by sub-editors, who tended to be more sober. (Though they too drank hard, it was usually when their shifts were completed. At most, they would allow themselves a few pints in mid-shift. Very occasionally, a sub or subs would go on spectacular benders, and complete mayhem would ensue.)

The other point, and this is harder to explain, is that many of these hard-drinking journalists were capable of writing well and fast against the clock. I sometimes saw John Pirie drink more or less all day. Then, at about six or seven in the evening, he'd send over 300 or 400 words of excellent, crisp, well-judged copy (and, as I have explained, it was often much more difficult to send over a few paragraphs than the journalistic equivalent of *War and Peace*).

But I have not elaborated on why journalists and pubs went together – and I'm not sure I can. I've heard it said that there was a similarity with police work: many journalists saw the grimier, grimmer, dirtier side of life, and drinking was a method of protecting yourself, blotting that out, seeing that you didn't become brutalised. Certainly, many of the police who consorted with journalists were very hard drinkers; but I'm not sure about this explanation.

There was also the question of stress. Sometimes, working in the most unlikely and unhelpful of contexts, piecing together all the strands of a complex story, making sure that you were not beaten by the opposition, simply getting the story right and all the details accurate – all this could be highly stressful, particularly if you were working against the clock. Deadlines are by definition very demanding.

There's another explanation, too. From the late 1950s onwards, until the middle of the Thatcher era, Britain – and particularly Scotland – was bedevilled by constant industrial disputes. Covering these disputes became a staple of journalism in all types of papers, tabloid and broadsheet, local and national. And the coverage often involved hanging around interminably, waiting forever for meetings in smoke-filled rooms or trade-union halls or even boardrooms to finish. This applied to industrial correspondents in particular, but to many other reporters as well.

You spent many hours simply waiting, and you never knew when the meeting was going to break up, with a dramatic resolution or – more likely – an escalation of the dispute. Sometimes, these meetings went on long into the night. You could wait in the streets, or you could wait in the pub. (And I know that, up until the mid-1970s, the pubs were supposed to close at 10pm – but, if the truth be told, many of them didn't. And, if the nearest pub would not let you in after ten, there was usually a local hotel that would.) And so the pub culture spread and became an integral part of the business.

And the drinking did not necessarily militate against hard work. Willie Kemp, the *Scotsman* sports editor in the 1960s and 1970s, ran a small and understaffed department. Night after night, he worked very hard. But, when he'd subbed his copy, written his headlines and drawn his page plans for the first edition, he went off to the Edinburgh Press Club for two or three, maybe just occasionally four, pints. Then he'd return for the second-edition changes, and he put in another ninety minutes or so before leaving shortly after midnight.

The final point I'd make is that it was not a myth that you picked up stories in pubs. Partly, this was because those who wanted to impart information knew that there were certain pubs where plenty of journalists could be found. Partly, it was because there was nowhere like a pub to get tongues loose.

❝❞

There was of course a downside – sometimes a very bleak downside. Too many journalists succumbed to alcoholism. Too many of them kept on drinking just to kid themselves that their lives were not wrecked. The pub culture could be cruel; it took its toll. And journalists are clannish; there was an easy, gregarious comfort to be found in drinking with your mates and colleagues, and it was far too easy for family men to ignore the seemingly tedious responsibilities of domesticity.

And, despite the intense competition between papers and the in-house rivalries between colleagues, there is a kind of crazy, glorious conviviality about press work that is hard to explain to outsiders. The Scottish novelist Allan Massie has been a prolific writer of book reviews, features and commentaries for the Scottish press over several decades. Yet Allan has written, with a certain wistfulness, that he never knew the urgency of late editions or the mingled camaraderie and rivalry of the newsroom. But I'd just add that, too often, that world of urgency and camaraderie could spill over into desperation or despair.

Having written that, most journalists were good at

looking after each other – through their charity, the Newspaper Press Fund, and through the National Union of Journalists. Ian Bruce, a great pub man, was for many years the father of the NUJ chapel on the *Herald*. Ian saw a crucial part of this role as looking after colleagues who were in danger of falling (sometimes literally) by the wayside. He was in some ways a kind of unpaid social worker. In this work, he was often supported by another fine colleague, Bob Jeffrey.

So – journalists drank too much, they fiddled their expenses, they mingled and inquired and laughed and listened and became frighteningly well informed, they wrote their (sometimes exceptionally good) copy, they lived and played and worked hard, they were at once gloriously idle and frenetically busy, they plied this difficult, demanding and dangerous trade, and always, always, they were aware of that insidious and deadly tyrant – the deadline.

8

Deadline

Ask most journalists to define news, and amazingly they will struggle. Cynics might aver that this is because modern newspapers carry very little actual news. (An American definition of a newspaper editor is: someone who is paid a lot of money to separate the wheat from the chaff, and then print the chaff.) My wife provides an effective and crisp definition: 'Something new that is of public interest'. When I was learning to be a journalist in Newcastle, I was told simply that news was information about very recent events. Another definition I was given in Newcastle was: 'News is something someone doesn't want in the paper. All the rest is advertising.' Of course, that is absurd, for the advertiser's competitors don't want his ads in the paper. But at least that definition suggests that there is something unsettling and even subversive about real news.

In the early 1970s, the *Scotsman* was changing rapidly, but the actual newsgathering routine was conservative and unimaginative. The key to the action, such as it was, consisted of The Diary, a vast, leather-bound tome which sat splendidly on a lectern alongside the news desk, where the news editor, Stuart Brown, and his deputy sat in their pomp. Diary jobs were marked up in advance in The Diary; they were jobs that could be predicted weeks, even months ahead – meetings of the Dean of Guild Court, that sort of thing. Late one night, a drunken sub-editor, fed up with the stodgy fare he was subbing, wandered over to The Diary and scrawled in huge writing over the diary page for the next day: 'Why don't you people get off your arses and chase some real news just for once?'

In those days, the *Scotsman* preferred to cover the obvious stories with scrupulous thoroughness. In 1971, I was the junior member of a team of three covering the General Assembly of the Church of Scotland. The two reporters who covered it during the day had immaculate shorthand. They took copious notes and produced long, verbatim reports of the proceedings. They had covered previous Assemblies and were conversant with the arcane procedures and the quasi-legal language that was used. I would go up to the Assembly Hall in the early evening to relieve them towards close of business; yet I was lucky, for sometimes that was when the best stories developed.

Indeed, I soon learned that, on the *Scotsman*, the best reporting shift was the last one, from 8pm until 3am. This was reserved for reporters of at least some aptitude and experience; if you completed three weeks of these shifts without mishap, you were entitled to an '823' tie (just a plain necktie with a motif of the numbers 823). I was rather pleased with myself when I got my 823 tie; it was a minor trophy, the marking of a rite of passage. I still have it at the bottom of a drawer. The 823 shift started with a visit to Leith Docks to check on the day's shipping movements. This could probably have been done by phone, but Stuart Brown felt it important to maintain daily contact with the harbour officials at the pilots' office. Then there were the calls, each hour, to the police, coastguards and fire and ambulance services. Even the *Scotsman* kept our contacts in these services happy with the occasional bottle of whisky or whatever, so there was no difficulty in getting a tip if something was happening.

My first reasonably big story on an 823 shift was a fire at a guesthouse in Portobello at about 2am. When I arrived, the *Express* were already there, inevitably; of the *Record* there was no sign. The *Express* reporter was worried about his deadline; it was almost last-edition time. But I knew that the *Scotsman* could take copy for its final edition until round about 3:30am if need be. In the event, the *Express* man could not file on time for this final edition, and I had the story to myself. It was a slow news night, and it got a good show on the front page.

It was only when I was reading it in the paper later that morning, with a certain satisfaction, that I suddenly realised, with a frisson of dismay, the full human significance of the story. I had reported on a fire in which two people had died. It was a tragedy, albeit a small one, as well as a story. I'd been wrapped up in doing the job, trying to get everything right, trying to do it professionally. I'd been insensitive. That is a tiny example of how newsgathering can make reporters hardened, or even callous.

Nowadays, it is very different. Newspapers rely more and more on agencies for the reporting of the likes of fires and industrial disputes, unless they are really major. And, as for predictable, planned Diary events like the Kirk's General Assembly, few of the actual proceedings are reported at all. Papers like the *Scotsman* used to clear at least a page in advance for thorough reports on each day of the Assembly; now the Kirk has no guarantee of any coverage at all. Indeed, there is far less reporting of what is actually said at any gathering. Journalists look for an angle, a follow-up; they want to flesh out some potential controversy, but not to report the actual proceedings. The same applies to the reporting of the Westminster Parliament, and also the Holyrood Parliament. The contemporary trend is to give more space and projection to sketchwriters and commentators than to the reporters who actually report what our legislators have said. I am slightly worried about this tendency in so far as it implies that journalists – sketchwriters and commentators – are more important than the elected representatives.

To be fair, newspapers have been moving in this direction for some time. It was quite a few years ago that the fine American journalist Joe Liebling averred: 'There are three type of journalist. The reporter, who reports what he sees. The interpretative reporter, who reports what he construes to be the meaning of what he sees. And the expert, who reports what he construes to be the meaning of what he has not seen.'

The decline in the reporting of what has actually been said is deprecated, in my view correctly, by Brian Wilson, the former Labour MP and minister, who in an earlier life was the founder of the *West Highland Free Press*. Brian says: 'I'm a great admirer of straight reporting. One of the ironies of the debate about spin is that the worst practitioners of spin are the newspapers. It's now endemic. I think it's partly the way that journalism is taught now. There always has to be an angle, there always has to be a first paragraph, which is a shock or a row or a furore or something like that. It has spread from the tabloids into the supposedly more serious newspapers. To me, one of the finest forms of journalism is verbatim reporting, actually chronicling what was said. The texture of the argument rather than interpretation of it. That is a very straightforward type of journalism that I think underpins the quality of great newspapers – and it is almost non-existent now in Scotland. The stories won't have come from actually going out and looking for something, and they won't have come from actually chronicling what people have said. To me, these are the two sources that real journalism and real quality come from.'

Despite the undoubted pertinence of these reflections, there is a tendency to overlook the sheer stodginess of some reporting in the 1960s and 1970s. Reporters with immaculate shorthand tended to have acute difficulty in isolating the key points in a long speech. They took down too much – and therefore, when they were going through page after page after page of notes later, they sometimes struggled to find the nub of the story. Another consideration was that some papers simply did not have the space to print paragraph after paragraph of verbatim reportage. In a tabloid format, such journalism was never appropriate anyway. The best tabloid journalist I knew, John Pirie of the *Daily Record*, was constantly looking for what he called 'the human-interest angle'. He mixed comment and reporting in a way that purists would regard as remiss; yet John was a respected journalist of integrity, and I never knew him distort anything.

A more cynical point is that many Scottish consumers of newspapers simply do not want to read extended accounts of the effusions of those whom they regard as windbags. They are conscious that they are living in a country that may well be over-governed. They have elected representatives in Europe, elected representatives at Holyrood, elected representatives at Westminster, elected representatives on the local council. Many people, particularly young people, forcefully tell me that they don't want to know what these people are *saying*; they want to know what they are *doing*.

And a final point here is that the rise and rise of the Internet does give those who are interested an alternative source of information about the proceedings in parliaments, assemblies and so on.

❛❜

The veteran Scottish journalist George Rosie reflects: 'It's been said that we'll soon be living in a global village. One of the characteristics of a village is personal gossip. I think the media are becoming more and more attuned to personal gossip, to personalities and general gossip. But I think a lot has been lost in this process. I think celebrity culture is a plague on newspapers. It makes me want to tear my shirt. It trivialises so much. You can't get a story unless there's a celebrity attached to it. There are so many interesting and important things out there, stories to be told, and you find page after page after page taken up with celebrity nonsense. That is one of the more unfortunate characteristics of the twenty-first-century Scottish press.'

John McGurk, the former editor of the *Scotsman*, says: 'As you mature as a journalist, you get away from the very popular human-interest stuff. As you mature in newspapers, you start to realise that there's some pretty trivial stuff you've been involved in, the stuff which doesn't really mean anything. It's titillation, it's trivia, it's a laugh. I think, as you mature, you start to realise that intelligent, thinking people want something much, much more than that.'

There is a lot of unease in these quotes. Compounding this unease is the belief that many big and powerful organisations, including governments and multinational businesses, now have exceptionally sophisticated press and PR operations, often staffed by former journalists, whose job it is to manipulate information and to package it for lazy journalists. This was not the case a couple of generations ago.

On the other hand, surely it is the job of the tenacious reporter to cut through all the spin and packaging? There used to be a breed of Scottish reporter who was both pugnaciously sceptical and persistent. Alan Cochrane of the *Daily Telegraph* describes this type: 'They always assume they're being told lies. They always think the worst of everyone. They always question and question and question what they're being told. I think these are very healthy instincts, and I've seen them in more Scottish reporters than in any other nationality. We do breed cantankerous journalists, and we've got to find a way of nourishing them. Unfortunately, I'm not sure if the current set-up in our indigenous press is all that interested in nurturing such people. Now people are looking for an easy life and, frankly, an easy buck. I'm afraid that the old hairy-arsed Scottish reporter might be on his way out.'

I hope he'll forgive me, but I reckon that an exemplar of this type of journalist is my old friend and colleague Murray Ritchie. Yet Murray has a lot of sympathy for contemporary journalists who are confronted with expensive and sophisticated spin machines. He says: 'Spin is a monster, and it stretches into government and into every aspect of business and public life. There are PR people and information officers and press officers and spin doctors who try to tell newspapers what to say and how to say it. It's very insidious, and it's difficult to resist because it can be very tempting to do the lazy thing and just take what the PR guy says and not see beyond what he's trying to tell you or how he's trying to influence you.'

These viewpoints point to a disaffection, which I have heard expressed by many consumers of newspapers as well as journalists, particularly in the past two or three years. In this context, it is interesting to note that most Scottish journalists now start their careers with some kind of formal training. Formerly, most training was done on the hoof, on the job, preferably on small local papers. And, significantly, many of these papers are doing better in the Scottish marketplace than the bigger and more self-important titles. Local papers are keenly read, not least because they supply good old-fashioned basic news, which is straightforwardly reported and presented.

The award-winning religious journalist Muriel Armstrong recalls her early days on the *Southern Reporter* forty years ago: 'The *Southern*, as it was simply known, was based in Selkirk, right in the middle of the high street. The editor was a chap called Willie Wilson who'd been a rear gunner in the RAF during the war and was still shaking a bit from the experience. He took his job as tutor to the new "girl on the *Southern*" very seriously. Your editor was your tutor, not just your boss. It does strike me nowadays that young reporters don't seem to understand the essence of a news story as I was taught it, namely that it does not have any comment in it at all unless it is attributed to a particular person. That much I remember – and the awful shorthand lessons.

'Our copy was punched out on fairly hefty typewriters in the reporters' room just off the caseroom. As the paper covered several counties which included small towns and a number of villages, the work was very varied, and involved attending everything from hunt balls to agricultural shows, town and county councils, various courts, and the Presbytery, which in these days was a source of good local stories. You soon built up your contacts in each town and village, and you relied on them. The Linotype machines were gas-fired, and the lead ingots were moved about the Borders from one paper to another. On press day, if there were any misprints on the front page, then a bash with what looked like a chisel on the lead was used to make a blot where the misspelling or whatever had occurred. It was very hard work and good fun. I never had a desire to head for a daily newspaper, though most of the trainees did. My chief reporter was called Jim Wightman. I met him in the press room of the General Assembly the day Margaret Thatcher addressed it. He was by then political editor of the *Daily Telegraph*. The pay then was £4 per week, going up to £6 when I became a member of the National Union of Journalists. It was possible to supplement income with lineage from the dailies (strictly forbidden of course), but that was mainly done from the telephone box out in the street.'

❛❜

In Chapter 2, I mentioned that Eric Mackay, shortly after he became editor of the *Scotsman* in 1972, decided to shake up the newsroom. He did this by appointing a group of specialist correspondents. In retrospect, it seems an obvious thing to do, but at the time on the *Scotsman* it was regarded as well nigh revolutionary, and it certainly annoyed the news desk – the news editor Stuart Brown, his deputy and their assistants. Although Mackay insisted that his new specialists should operate through the news desk, Stuart was worried – to some extent presciently – that he would lose control of a significant part of his newsgathering empire; the specialists would want to work independently.

The initiative rapidly bore fruit, for the specialists were soon providing regular exclusives. The problem was to make these exclusives significant for the wider readership, and not just the specialist constituency. It became a convention that a specialist should bring in at least a couple of reasonable exclusives each week. The best way to do this was to nurture a wide range of contacts who trusted you.

As the newly appointed education correspondent, one of the first contacts I developed was the young student rector of Edinburgh University, one Gordon Brown. Gordon was the second student rector; but, unlike the first, he availed himself of his constitutional right to chair the university court, its governing body. The court met once a month – and, apart from senior university figures like the principal and the university secretary, its membership comprised a group of the great and the good, judges and the like. The main decisions of the court, until then, had been communicated to the wider public by means of a rather ponderous and evasive communiqué, and occasional press conference – two days after the court had met. The university was very much in control; it decided how much information was to be provided about the court's deliberations and its decisions. There was, for example, never the whiff of a suggestion that decisions had not been agreed unanimously.

Gordon and I took to having a couple of pints immediately after the meetings concluded. He told me everything that had happened. This was a time of constant controversy in higher education, of student militancy and industrial unrest among the non-academic staff and even some of the academic staff. So, there was plenty of meat – some strong stories that the university authorities were not best pleased to see splashed all over the *Scotsman* the next day. Soon, the then principal Sir Hugh Robson was complaining bitterly and regularly to Eric Mackay. To his credit, Mackay swatted the complaints aside. He was never one to kowtow to the Edinburgh establishment in any way.

And so the *Scotsman*'s approach to newsgathering slowly changed, and the long verbatim reports began to disappear. I regret that aspect of the change; the *Scotsman*'s news-reporting had been constipated, but on the other hand it provided a record of what people had said – many of them articulate people with something significant to say – which was both useful and dignified.

❛❜

It used to be thought that the quickest way to an editor's chair was to have a precocious career as a sub-editor; that is, as a production man. Eric Mackay was a sub through and through, and he hated having to write anything. Yet, I and many others always felt that working on the production side of newspapers was ultimately no substitute for getting out into the field, onto the streets, into the bars and the smoke-filled rooms, meeting people and cultivating contacts.

Fidelma Cook recalls her early days on the *Daily Record*: 'The sad thing, or it can be a good thing, is that every single person a good reporter meets, no matter where or how, socially or otherwise, is a potential contact. In the 1970s, when you worked on a national paper you were considered the cream – you didn't expect, as somebody now would, to come straight out of a news agency and be working on a national paper. Bless them, but it shouldn't be like that. It should be people who've really been tested and learned and done their time in the districts and know where to go and have contacts. And the people on both the *Record* and the *Express* had incredible contacts. Paying for a story – now that's a very modern phenomenon. It was a badge of honour not to pay for a story. Your expertise was to get people to talk to you and hopefully to trust you. Television changed things for reporters. Suddenly, people were seeing people saying "No comment", so you'd go to the meanest house and it would be Nae Comment, hen.'

Tabloid reporters in particular had to develop a variety of crafty techniques to get people to talk. Fidelma recalls: 'The hard men would go up to the door, particularly if it was a murder – and we did a lot of them in Glasgow in those days – and the hard men would go to the door first. And it was always right at the top of a tenement, it was never on the first floor. And you'd hear the swearing, the yelling; some of the hard men have been punched down the stairs, that wasn't uncommon. And then another one would go up and try … And then I'd go in. And I'd press the bell, and out would come this bear, you know, Ya F—ing … and I'd just look up and say I'm so, so sorry. I'm from the *Daily Record* and it's my first job. Can I just pretend to stand here for a little while? I think it's awful what they're doing, I wouldn't do it, but if I … And they'd look at you and they'd say, ya poor wee soul. Oh hen, come in.'

Of course mishaps, even disasters, could happen in more genteel contexts. John McGurk remembers: 'It was a bit like being a salesman. You knock on the door of the local WRVS, the local old folk's club and the local ministers. I went to this minister, and I was trying to get a story, and on his sideboard there's a picture of Ken Dodd, who was a pretty popular comedian at the time. To try and break the ice, I say: Ken Dodd, is that someone you know? And he looked at me and looked at the picture, looked back at me and said: "That's a photograph of my wife".'

Anne Simpson of the *Herald* reflects on the need for sensitivity: 'Where you worry about exploiting people is when you are walking into a situation of grief. Very often, you've got to sit there for a long time listening to someone talking, and you've got to be careful that you're not pushing them into becoming tearful just for the sake of being able to put that in your story. And if you're working for a news editor who wants the outpouring of grief in a kind of lurid way, you've got to stand up and fight and say no, that's kind of mawkish.'

Anne reckons that the excitement of newsgathering is the feeling of being at the hub of things that can be moving very fast. 'Even on quite small stories, there's very often a more interesting story than the one you go out to cover. In the course of conversation, you find that something is leading onto something else. You have to have a basic curiosity about people to be able to draw them out without exploiting them.'

The growth of electronic media has of course meant that newspapers are no longer the kings of the domain of news. John McGurk says: 'Newspapers no longer break stories as such. They do break exclusive stories, but these stories are exclusive for all of five minutes. They're picked up by television, by radio, by websites. And, by the morning, the story which has been broken by the newspaper has been broken by one of the broadcast media. Broadcasters are very good at stealing from newspapers.'

❛ ❜

The three key areas of Scottish life, before and after devolution, which are distinctively Scottish – i.e. non-British – are the law, education and religion. I canvassed the opinion of a key senior player in each area in an attempt to track whether the coverage by the Scottish press had improved or deteriorated over the years.

To discuss the law, I turned to Douglas Mill, secretary and chief executive of the Law Society of Scotland for the past nine years, and formerly a solicitor in Paisley. Douglas told me: 'In terms of our separate legal system, you have to ask: who exactly speaks for it? That is a problem for the Scottish press. Most of the constituent parts – the judiciary, the Crown Office, the Faculty of Advocates and so on – have been rather slow to recognise the importance of the Scottish press. But, having said that, I'm afraid that, overall, I suspect that the quality of the coverage has probably declined. For example, very few papers have dedicated court reporters now. Legal affairs are increasingly covered by general reporters who have little knowledge or understanding of the legal background. And there is a gross over-concentration on the criminal law. Scots law is a key part of our heritage, and it is in serious danger of being eroded. There is not a sufficient understanding in our press of what has made us distinctive – of the separateness of our legal system. There are commercial pressures from south of the Border (and from Europe also, to a lesser extent) for a unified system of law. There is still a profound respect for Scots law abroad, and in the US in particular, and I don't see this reflected in the Scottish press. Our newspapers are not picking this concern up – and they probably would have, twenty or thirty years ago.'

For an overview of the Scottish press's educational coverage, I turned to Fred Forrester, who was a teacher in secondary schools in Glasgow before embarking on a long and high-profile career as a senior official with the

EIS. For the past decade, he has been a commentator and consultant on Scottish educational affairs. Fred told me: 'I think Scottish education is still covered well in our serious press, perhaps less so in the popular press. I'd say the quality of the education correspondents is the key factor. The *Herald* and the *Scotsman* have specialist correspondents, and also dedicated education pages. They provide fair coverage for the specialist and also for the average reader. The popular press, these days, is rather less concerned with educational matters. The popular press has definitely gone rapidly downmarket.'

What seems to me the most crucial area of all is religious affairs. I hope I do not write that as any kind of religious zealot, but rather as someone who understands the crucial part that religion still plays in Scotland, even in these aggressively secular times. After all, the Church of Scotland has around half a million members. Many of them are pretty passive and not exactly lively participants in the Kirk. But the figure is still impressive for a country of just five million people, even though it used to be much higher. The more impressive statistic is the 40,000 elders in the Kirk. (Elder is not a word I like; some of them are undoubtedly elderly, but many are middle-aged, and a surprising number are actually quite young.) An elder is ordained, and is by definition a committed, active member. What political party in Scotland comes anywhere near having 40,000 committed members?

Ron Ferguson, a columnist with both the *Herald* and the *Press and Journal*, was minister of St Magnus Cathedral in Orkney and before that a minister in Easterhouse, Glasgow. He was also leader of the Iona Community. And, before any of that, he worked as a reporter with the *Edinburgh Evening News* in the 1960s. Ron recalls: 'In the 1960s, coverage of religious affairs in Scotland was substantial. The coverage, mind you, was almost entirely restricted to Christianity, and the Church of Scotland in particular got a lot of column inches. The *Evening News* ran a weekly religious round-up, edited by Bruce Cannon; and, when it came to the Kirk's General Assembly, at least two reporters would be present for the paper every day. Religion was treated as big news. The *Scottish Daily Express* was famed for its campaign in the late 1950s against bishops in the Kirk – that made front-page banner headlines. Inconceivable today! Both the *Herald* and the *Scotsman* had religious-affairs specialists, and their coverage showed the benefit of an extensive network of contacts. In later years, Stewart Lamont on the *Herald* acted as both a reporter and a pundit, producing several exclusives. What is noticeable now is the number of howlers about religion in Scotland. One notorious *Scotsman* heading talked about a Scottish vicar – who turned out to be a minister of the Church of Scotland. Not only was the reporter ignorant of Scottish religious terminology, but also the night editor failed to pick it up. That would have been impossible twenty years ago. Although memberships of the mainstream churches have declined dramatically, religious issues still create much interest – as evidenced by the letters pages of the *Herald* and the *Scotsman*. What is missing in the coverage is the authority of informed analysis, and familiarity with the subject matter.'

Peter Kearney, director of the Catholic Media Office in Glasgow, told me that the coverage of religious affairs in the Scottish press had become increasingly superficial. 'Too often, only rows make the headlines, leaving denominations pressured by a combative media culture into denouncing, decrying or deploring. Admittedly, church attendances have fallen quite markedly – not to be confused with levels of interest in religion and spirituality, which remain high – but then so has attendance at football matches, and turnout at elections. These latter trends have not been accompanied by a corresponding drop in press coverage of football or politics. Editors seem to be saying: interest in religion, measured by attendance, is dropping, and therefore coverage should also reduce. This contrasts strongly with the line on politics, which seems to be: interest in politics, measured by turnout and membership of parties and trade unions, is falling – therefore coverage should increase.'

❛❜

Scottish newspapers are of course much fatter than they were forty years ago; pagination has increased enormously. In what older journalists regard as the glory days, the newspapers tended to come in one section, and one section only, and there was no colour printing. The papers were thin, monochromatic and rather smudgy. There was far less reading in them. Yet there was far more actual news. And the papers were devoured with more care and attention, I'm certain of that.

The trend away from good old-fashioned news has been partly driven by marketing executives, who tend to have too much influence in newspaper offices these days. They sometimes appear to be obsessed with attracting younger readers and so-called aspirational readers whose main concern is apparently 'lifestyle', whatever that may or may not be.

Editors used to operate on a heady mixture of experience, flair and instinct; now they are constantly advised, if not actually bullied, by focus groups and market researchers and audience surveys. It takes a strong and confident editor to resist all this pressure; but I do note that the obsession with gaining younger readers does not seem to be succeeding. There is nothing worse than middle-aged or elderly editorial executives trying to produce copy and features specifically aimed at younger readers. The results are at best patronising, at worst absurd.

In terms of news, newspapers – at both ends of the market – are losing their authority. In some respects, they are no longer really 'news' papers at all. Joan Burnie, the veteran *Record* journalist, puts it bluntly: 'Scots no longer get their news from the newspapers, it's as simple as that. Scots don't trust newspapers any more, as they undoubtedly did through the 1960s and 1970s. Nowadays, they get their prejudices from their newspapers, but other sources provide their news.'

That is a bleak view. To counter it, I present some sentences from David Ross, the *Herald*'s long-serving Highland correspondent. He is in effect writing his own job description. I think it illustrates what remains valuable and important about much Scottish daily journalism. 'My patch stretches from Unst, the most northerly of the Shetland Islands, to the Mull of Kintyre right down at the south end of Kintyre. It is an area the size of Belgium, but with a total population of just 435,000. The themes of landownership, remoteness and sparsity of population underpin many of the stories that make it to the Scottish national news agenda. Along with the Gaelic language and the unrivalled physical environment, they mean that the Highlands and Islands are still seen as Scotland's magical lands, to where many urban Scots proudly trace their ancestry. Despite that, the Highlands and Islands can be the stuff of caricature, even in the Scottish newspapers in the twenty-first century. Highland Presbyterianism can still be openly ridiculed, a treatment Scottish journalists would hesitate to accord to Roman Catholicism and would not contemplate for Islam. And will the Mod ever lose the Whisky Olympics tag? Partly as a consequence, the Highland correspondent cannot help but see himself as an advocate for his area. Without such trust, he could not perform his dual function: to explain the Highlands and Islands to the rest of Scotland, all the while striving to make his newspaper relevant to a local readership.'

‘ ’

It is fashionable to deplore the lack of serious investigative journalism in the Scottish press. This complaint is exaggerated. I was personally delighted when, in 2000, the *Herald* business writer Simon Bain was named Scotland's Journalist of the Year for his well-researched and brave exposé of petrol price-fixing in the north of Scotland. Work like this is rare, but it does appear from time to time in the Scottish papers. And, in these more frugal days, you have to remember that there is a big risk in investigative journalism. Not just a legal risk, though that usually looms, but also a budgetary risk. You are asking one, two or even three reporters to work on a story that they will probably need at least a couple of weeks, maybe more, to make stand up. And what if they don't succeed, through no fault of their own? You've lost all that time and money.

It also has to be noted that the Scottish press's attempts at creating special investigative units have not always been blessed with conspicuous success. I mentioned that the *Scotsman*, so often prescient in the 1960s, set up an investigation unit called Close Up. There was nothing wrong with the calibre of the journalists – Gus Macdonald, Magnus Magnusson and David Kemp. But their methods were regarded as a bit wild, and the unit was soon disbanded. Later, the *Scotsman's* long-serving editor, Eric Mackay, rather scathingly remarked of his investigative reporter George Hume: 'All those flat stones lifted up, and the only things that came out were a few wee slaters'.

In 1981, Charles Wilson, perhaps the finest Scottish editor of modern times in terms of sheer mastery of newsgathering, set up a special-investigations unit as part of his new *Sunday Standard*. The team he assembled produced some reasonable stories, but nothing earth-shattering.

❛❜

Finally, the topic that has dominated the Scottish public agenda, one way or another, for almost forty years is of course devolution. As I have tried to show, it was to a large extent the invention not so much of the Scottish people but of the Scottish press, and the *Scotsman* in particular. The debate that the *Scotsman* started in the late 1960s led, after many twists and turns, to the establishment of the Scottish Parliament in 1999. This was a fundamental and authentically historic development in the life of the Scottish nation.

Ironically, it was delivered by a prime minister who did not seem all that enthused by the need for constitutional change. Peter Riddell, the highly respected chief political commentator of the London *Times*, has noted that the most lasting legacy of the Blair premiership is likely to be the area in which Blair himself has shown least interest: the constitution. More importantly, Riddell has identified two crucial aspects of the devolved settlement, which have, unfortunately, not always been reflected by the Scottish press. The first is that the Scotland Act explicitly states that the UK (Westminster) Parliament is and will remain sovereign in *all* matters. The second crucial point is that the powers of the Scottish Parliament established by the Scotland Act derive from Westminster, not from the Scottish people.

This is the true constitutional position; but many Scots remain erroneously convinced that the new Parliament reflects the claim of the Scottish Constitutional Convention in 1988 that the Scottish people had a sovereign right to determine the form of government suited to their needs. The Scottish press, or influential parts of it, could be criticised for a lack of clarity in dealing with these issues. But more germane here, in the context of the discussion of the reporting of news, is how the new Scottish Parliament – the biggest Scottish story in a long time – has itself been reported. My personal view is that it has not been badly reported, but there has perhaps been too much commentary and sketchwriting, and not enough old-fashioned verbatim reporting of debates and committee work.

I asked the television journalist and Scottish political historian David Torrance for his views. He said: 'After the referendum of 1979, devolution vanished for a year or so as a political issue. The *Scotsman* had kept it going for a long period before that. The *Herald* had only flirted with devolution in the 1970s; but then, into the 1980s, it picked up the issue and embraced it. I think the crucial figures as that decade developed were Arnold Kemp, editor of the *Herald*, and Donald Dewar, who kept the devolution cause alive in the Labour Party during the long years of opposition. And, when it became clear in the 1990s that devolution was finally going to become reality, expectations were over-raised. I definitely blame the print media for this. Far more than the politicians, they exaggerated expectations as to what devolution could deliver. Then, when the Parliament did arrive in 1999, the reporting was not always of the best. Sometimes a kind of pack mentality ruled, and this became more important than considerations of an individual story's merits. I'd even say that a bit of a clique developed, and to some extent that dictated the coverage. Of course, some journalists stood apart from that, and I'd commend them. I'd single out in particular Ian Swanson of the *Edinburgh Evening News*.'

My own perspective on these comments is that, although what David Torrance calls the pack mentality did probably exist for a time, most of the political reporters worked hard to provide fair and authoritative coverage of the infant Parliament's deliberations. The problem probably lay higher up the newspaper hierarchies. One or two newspapers were ill-disposed to the new Parliament from the start. For whatever reason, the Parliament has been, thus far, a grievous disappointment to many Scots.

The Scottish Parliament's presiding officer, George Reid, himself a former journalist, delivered a stringent attack on negative reporting of the fledgling institution when he addressed the 2006 congress of the International Press Institute. He complained about colourful and erroneous stories, and reflected on a press culture consisting of a relentlessly competitive market and increasingly populated with freelances who had to 'sex up' their stories if they were going to sell them. Stressing that devolution had certainly not been a disaster, he conceded that the new Parliament had been dogged by reporting of its costly and controversial building.

Yet, important as the new Parliament is, parliamentary reporting is of necessity a fairly refined and rarefied kind of reporting. The real reporting of news, and the way that so many Scottish journalists learned it, was not at all refined. I leave the last word with Anne Simpson: 'I seem to have this memory of it always being a dark rainy night. And when you did find a phone, wind would be whistling through the panes of glass that had been smashed. And the box usually smelled of urine ...'

9

Crazy to Solemn –
A Daily Progression

There is a craziness about the press, and the Scottish press in particular. If you worked in a Scottish newspaper office, you sensed that madness was never too far away. Fidelma Cook reminisces about the legendary *Record* editor Bernie Vickers: 'There were always mad things happening when he was around. The Muppets were a very popular television series, and it was decided that our readers would like to win Muppet puppets. So, this stack of Muppet puppets arrived, and Bernard insisted that they be delivered to his office, because he had a great fondness for the Muppet puppets. And he opened the box that contained God knows how many – and that was after lunch. He came down the hall with armfuls of Muppets and insisted that every head of department vacate their chair. And they were replaced by a Muppet. And he only addressed the Muppets for the rest of the day. Occasionally, the head of department would answer for the Muppets – but Bernard would say he was speaking to the Muppet.'

Scottish journalism was always full of pranks and mischief. When Frank Frazer was setting off from the *Scotsman*'s Glasgow office to his first big oil conference at Houston, the photographer Gordon Rule – one of the most relentless practical jokers I can recall – stuck three unrolled condoms to the outside of Frank's newly purchased and rather swish travelling bag. I can still see Frank, a big and cheerful man, standing and grinning as he waved goodbye to us at the door of the Gordon Street office, clutching his bag, unaware of the condoms swaying gently in the wind.

Press conferences, and especially pompous or self-important speakers, always gave the hacks a chance to be a bit cheeky or mischievous and to puncture any self-serving would-be orators. I once attended a news conference held by a bunch of educationists who had earlier held a weekend meeting of what they regarded as momentous import. There were interminable references from the chairman to the Queensferry agenda, the Queensferry resolutions and even, heaven help us, the Queensferry protocols. Eventually I interrupted, saying I needed elucidation on an important point. Was this North or South Queensferry? Not a particularly witty intervention, I grant you – but the other reporters present guffawed loudly, and thereafter the chairman rather lost his way.

The fine *Herald* writer Willie Hunter moonlighted for many years as a sportswriter on a certain Sunday paper. When Willie at last decided that he did not want to file any more Saturday-afternoon football reports from the likes of Boghead or Cappielow or Stark's Park, he played a final mischievous game of his own: he ensured that every single sentence in his last report contained a cliché. The intro actually read: 'This was a game of two halves'. That evening, the sports editor of the Sunday paper contacted Willie urgently. Willie expected an admonition – but the sports editor was ecstatic. He told Willie he'd never read such eloquent copy. Willie could have a staff job, there and then. He could name his salary.

And so it goes on. But the craziest thing of all is the immediacy. Most of this book is about daily as opposed to weekly or Sunday journalism. Producing a daily newspaper is a unique privilege. Each working day, you are producing a wholly new product. Its shelf life is laughably brief, it is almost instantly perishable – but, for the few hours of its relevant glory, it is an impressive and in its own way complex artefact, produced against the clock. And, if you are editing a daily paper, and you have a bad day or night, and the product isn't as good as it should be – and goodness knows, that happens often enough – at least you know you will be starting completely anew the next morning. This relentless twenty-four-hour ratchet is at once refreshing and absurdly demanding. It is no wonder that daily newspaper journalists, and in particular editorial executives, are not the most patient or reflective of people.

But the twenty-four-hour ratchet militates against any long- or even mid-term thinking. Ask the average daily newspaper editor to think strategically, and he'll mention next week. When Gus Macdonald was considering me for the *Herald* editorship, he asked me where I thought the *Herald* would be positioned in ten years' time. Privately, I thought: 'That's a real smart-ass question', though of course I didn't say so. But, later, I realised that it was an important and good question. Too many people in the industry are so intensely caught up in the exigencies – exhilarating and stretching as they are – of daily production that they cannot think beyond tomorrow. Add to this crazy immediacy the extreme pressures of competition in an exceptionally tough marketplace, and you have a dangerous mix that constantly militates against reflection. Sometimes, I think the whole industry needs to calm down and become a little more thoughtful.

Having written that, it would be wrong to present journalistic life as a constant round of bruising, frenetic, deadline-driven crises. There used to be, and maybe still is, a soft and surprisingly dreamy side to Scottish journalism. Some of the most unworldly people you could imagine used to inhabit Scottish newsrooms, and maybe one or two of them are still around, relics of a more eccentric era. And, although most of the Scottish journalists I have known have been superb at working under pressure, there were always one or two who were passengers. In the *Scotsman* newsroom in the early 1970s, some of the news sub-editing was ponderous and dreadfully sluggish; it was the frenetic few who got the paper out. And, at that time, some of the copy in the softer areas of papers like the *Scotsman* and the *Glasgow Herald* was both precious and bland, lacking any tension or interest. Some of the executives in charge were laggardly and unimaginative.

In the mid-1970s, Anne Simpson arrived at the *Glasgow Herald* from the *Yorkshire Post*. She was the paper's new women's editor, and she had the brief of developing a public voice for women in Scotland. So, here she was in Glasgow, supposedly this most raucous, demanding and hard-bitten of newspaper environments. Anne recalls: 'There was nothing for the next day's paper on my first day. I'd thought there'd be some subjects in hand. They said, well, there may be some articles in that drawer – and so I opened it, and the first two articles I came to were a nice essay called "Collecting Old Spoons" and another one which was "Ornamental Things to Do with Autumn Leaves".'

The many Scottish journalists who trained with the old-fashioned Dundee newspaper house of DC Thomson (which also produced magazines and comics) have plenty of tales to tell of a kind of soft, time-warped eccentricity. Most of them moved on to a harder, coarser world in more mainstream journalism; but, looking back, they are not dismissive of the paternalistic, insulated world in which they found themselves as they set out on the great adventure. Dorothy-Grace Elder, a rare heroine of the *Scottish Daily News* saga, was once being interviewed for a job in Geneva with the UN. 'I started going on about how I'd been with the *Herald* and the BBC, and I was poshing it up – and then the guy asked, and so where did you start? And I said DC Thomson. He said: "Dundee? Why didn't you tell me in the first place? DC Thomson, the Harvard for hacks. We've never had a bad one yet from DC Thomson."'

Dorothy-Grace remembers the paternalism and the constant eccentricity at the DC Thomson offices. 'The Thomson family? It was Mr Harold, Mr That, Mr This. I remember at one stage some of the top bosses were wearing mittens. Yes, mittens. They were the sign of the top management, because in the winter days they were showing an example to the staff of keeping warm without turning the heating up. But, you know, out of that came a lot of damn good journalists. We were not pampered as youngsters – anything but. I think a bit of early humiliation helps, because if you're humiliated when you are older, it's much worse.'

Julie Davidson arrived at DC Thomson aged 18, to work as a sub-editor on magazines. 'I was only vaguely conscious that the company refused to let you join a union. I was not politicised then, and I accepted it. Later, I reflected that it was disgraceful that they did not allow any unionised staff on the premises. I looked back and saw an autocratic, patriarchal organisation. Later still, I look back again, and now I see a work environment that was very benign. There was a genuine concern for the employees. They really tried to help young employees in finding accommodation, for example. Even if they tended to send the young girls to the Church of Scotland hostel on Constitution Hill – it was known as the virgins' retreat. We worked hard, we worked on Christmas Day, there was never any overtime, women were paid less than men even if they were doing the same job, there was absolutely no frivolity, you had no access to outside phones, your timekeeping had to be spot-on. There were even stickers on the phones, which were for internal use only, telling you that you had to speak softly and pick up the phone with the words "Yes, please?" Being anarchic, I used to bellow: "Hello?" But the Thomson family cared for their employees. A certain amount of pastoral work, informal counselling and so on, took place. There was sincere concern for the welfare of the staff, particularly the younger staff.'

❝❞

Craziness, eccentricity, mischief, softness as well as hardness; another component in the heady mix was sentimentality. Journalists were often emotional, occasionally given to over-the-top maudlin excess. Sometimes, the supposedly hardest exemplars of the trade were the most mawkish. Journalists do farewell parties like no other group of people I know. I don't wish to dwell on this aspect of the business; some of it is downright silly. But, to illustrate the point, I will confess, perhaps inviting ridicule, that I was appalled when the venerable old Scotsman building on North Bridge, Edinburgh, a building in which I spent eleven very happy years, became a luxury hotel. I was only invited to this hotel once, and I never want to return to it. Somehow, and this is not wholly rational, I felt physically sick when I witnessed what had become of the rooms in which I used to work and in which newspapers were produced, night after night. Somehow, I felt the building had become defiled, debased.

In the summer of 2000, the Scottish Media Group, owners of the *Herald*, of which I was then editor, moved to a new custom-built plant at the top of Renfield Street, Glasgow. This entailed the evacuation of that extraordinary building in Albion Street, the 'black Lubyanka' which had only existed for seventy years yet had been the home of many papers. These titles, redolent of so much sweaty, sticky human endeavour, so much success and failure, included the *Evening Citizen*, the *Evening Times*, the short-lived *Sunday Standard*, the even shorter-lived *Scottish Daily News*, the infant *Sunday*

Herald, the *Glasgow Herald* and of course the greatest of them all, the *Scottish Daily Express*.

I'd been heavily involved in the detailed planning of the new Renfield Street building and the arrangements for the move. It was not until the very last day of work in that remarkable temple of journalism in Albion Street that the enormity of what was going on suddenly hit me. So many ghosts and memories were being left behind. And so, late on that glorious summer evening of Friday, 28 July 2000, I prowled round all the floors of the building, searching for somewhere quiet to spend ten minutes or so, gently communing with the many ghosts. But the building was in a state of mayhem: not only was the final newspaper to come out of Albion Street in the throes of production, but also workmen and contractors were everywhere, engaged in last-minute packing and boxing and dismantling and clearance and all the noisy activities connected with a removal on a grand scale.

At last, I found a haven in – of all places – the boardroom, up on the fourth floor. I found some peace there, with the late sun pouring through the big western window high above the trees of the old Ramshorn graveyard. I sat by the long table where I'd been so often over the previous years, attending meeting after meeting, sometimes acrimonious meetings about budget overspends and production slippages, sometimes heady and exciting meetings about new supplements or editions or projects.

More importantly, I thought of the building itself and all the characters who'd worked in it – all the camaraderie, the nonsense, the drunkenness, the good times, the bad times. Monarchs and prime ministers had visited it, as had Muhammad Ali, the supreme sporting hero of the twentieth century. It had been conceived and built and presided over by the greatest proprietor of them all, the larger-than-life Max Aitken, Lord Beaverbrook, who had himself worked there in its early days. Much later, another larger-than-life but disastrously flawed proprietor, Robert Maxwell, had also worked there. The finest Scottish foreign correspondent of the twentieth century, James Cameron, had learned his trade in the building, working as a down-table sub-editor, 'haunted by considerations of doom', as he wrote in his autobiography.

And so I thought of the literally thousands of journalists and printers and all the others who had worked in the building. I thought of the japes, the joy of a good paper, the despair of a bad one, the tension and anger and laughter, all the zany exploits of the past – and, above all, I thought of the sheer unremitting professionalism of those who had produced so many editions of such different and distinctive papers, and their constant battles against the clock. So many stories, so much effort, so many memories.

As I write this, the Albion Street building is being converted into luxury apartments. A luxury hotel in North Bridge, Edinburgh, and luxury apartments in Albion Street, Glasgow. I'm not impressed. But then there's no luxury like nostalgia, and I guess pressmen are world-class when it come to sumptuous, heart-aching nostalgia.

❛❜

A significant problem in journalism, and Scottish journalism in particular, was an incestuousness, a certain clannishness. This is perhaps less the case nowadays, when much newspaper production is routinely left to casual staff, and short-term contracts abound. In the past, to become a journalist in Scotland was to become one of a select breed. The sense of being different and apart from the considerations and concerns of normal humanity was particularly nurtured on the *Scottish Daily Express*, but it pervaded the whole gamut of newspapers.

Crazy to Solemn – A Daily Progression

There was this general feeling in Scottish journalism that you had joined a club. You belonged to a tight (perhaps the wrong word) cluster of colleagues and friends and rivals. If you belonged to this somewhat self-regarding world, you had a special raffish status conferred on you, and outsiders were excluded. Journalists would not only work with each other, they would also drink and party and even holiday together. Scottish journalists too often felt and behaved as if they belonged to a caste apart.

The downside of this, obviously enough, was an inbred arrogance, which could spill into disdain for non-journalists. Sometimes, this manifested itself in an insecure and beleaguered mindset, which I hope I always resisted. I rarely encountered this mindset on the *Herald*, but I can recall one instance. When I was deputy editor of the paper in 1991, I was instrumental in hiring the late Robin Cook as a guest racing tipster, with a weekly column. Robin was by far the most impressive and forensic parliamentary debater of his generation. He was at that time regarded as an assiduous but rather austere opposition MP, a bit of a cold fish. I knew of his genuine interest in the turf, and I think his *Herald* racing column helped to give him a more human and rounded public image.

There was some resentment about this hiring on the sports desk. There was a belief that the notion of a high-profile politician tipster was both a gimmick and a stunt. Well, undoubtedly it was, but Robin knew what he was writing about and proved to be a tipster worth following, though it did take several weeks before he managed to pick a winner. More importantly, he emerged as a commentator of authority on the wider racing scene. But the internal unease lingered, simply because he wasn't a journalist, one of our select freemasonry. Robin himself eventually broke down this suspicion by turning out to be unexpectedly affable on his occasional visits to the office. He also proved a scrupulous and timeous provider of copy, and that was appreciated.

In a frivolous footnote to this, I was delighted that, shortly after I became editor of the *Herald* in 1997, I was able to place on the front page, in the first announcement of the early Cabinet appointments, following New Labour's landslide victory, the immortal lines: *Foreign Secretary – Robin Cook (His racing tips are on page 41)*. That strapline gave me enormous pleasure. Robin manfully carried on providing his column for about six months, though he forfeited his (modest) fee as soon as he became a Minister of the Crown. Indeed, much of the work was by now being done by his son Christopher. But Robin's name still appeared above the copy. Eventually, Robin phoned me and said he really could continue no longer. I suspect, though I have no proof of this, that he was leaned on by Foreign Office mandarins, who did not think that the Foreign Secretary should be providing racing tips for a newspaper. Robin's racing journalism was a success; his copy had insight and freshness, and his column was talked about. Yet the initial reaction, within the *Herald*, was one of suspicion.

I have never liked this marginally insidious tendency for journalists to try to ring-fence their own fiefdom. It must be said that some of the best copy in newspapers comes from outsiders. Readers' letters are often, if not always, a case in point. My old friend Iain Thorburn, when he was a sub-editor on the *Evening Citizen* in Albion Street, had the chore of selecting the daily star letter, which carried a small monetary prize. Iain said that the variety and invention and concision of the offerings put the paper's highly paid feature-writers to shame.

Another example. We used to run on the *Herald* a major weekly essay by a non-journalist. The standard of submissions was exceptionally high. And, as I recalled earlier, the best writing I ever came across in the Scottish press was by a non-journalist, the politician/academic John P. Mackintosh. So, journalists have a tendency to be clannish, and to be too protective of their own shop. But now I suspect that, with the rise of so-called citizens' journalism, things are moving far too rapidly in the opposite direction.

In the glory years, the 1950s and 1960s and 1970s, television only very gradually emerged as a threat to the imperious sway of the career print journalist. The Internet, freesheets and other threats to this happy but smug fiefdom were as yet unthought of. Of course, there were capricious proprietors; newspapers sometimes shut down suddenly, and union power was abused – but, in the domain of news, the print reporter was king. Nowadays, as I say, the newspaper reporter's job is under threat as never before.

One of the key components in the Scottish press in the era that this book celebrates was the sub-editor. He (it was almost always a he) worked behind the scenes, often on a back shift, and tended to be a more sedulous, less boozy and less rakish figure than his reporting counterpart. Subbing was not exactly glamorous work, and the subs tended to be modest men whose style was effective rather than flamboyant. Admittedly, some of them were ambitious and went on to become fine editors. But, for the most part, they worked away in fairly dreary back-of-house environments, and they were not touched with the bravado or even the arrogance which were often the defining characteristics of their newsgathering writing colleagues. And they were reluctant to go down the rocky road of self-promotion.

But, when it came to their basic tasks, the copy-editing, the proof-reading, the headline-writing and the page-planning, most of these subs were meticulous, thorough and model professionals. Too often, they were looked down on by those who were on the road or in the street (or the pub). The subs may not have been characters, they were

169

certainly not larger than life, and their many virtues could be categorised as worthy, even a little boring. They were rarely sloppy; they maintained consistent standards of accuracy and rigour. And they were indispensable.

Their raw material was the copy from the reporters, the specialists, the sportswriters and the feature-writers. These writing journalists did of course sometimes produce copy that sang – golden words, magical phrases. Usually, the copy was tightly written and competent. But, from time to time, they also produced copy that was sloppy, inaccurate, over-subjective, even – very occasionally – downright illiterate or nonsensical. They knew they would be rescued. The unsung heroes on the subs' benches knocked the bad words into shape.

Now we have this new and dangerous world of blogs, websites, chatrooms, forums, gossip factories and so on. The new Internet era is about access to all – and that is superficially to be welcomed; it is democratic. And, in a way, the press deserves this development because, as I say, pressmen were too jealous of their closed-shop status, too confident that they could always keep the outsiders well excluded, that they had some God-given monopoly on news and information.

Yet anarchy beckons. The question is simple: who is to prevent the dissemination and circulation of malice, propaganda, spite, rumour and innuendo? Or, to put it another way, where are these experienced and careful sub-editors to provide a fail-safe, a long stop? Of course, it would be laughable to pretend that, in the golden age I have been celebrating, newspapers were bereft of propaganda or inaccuracy or extreme subjectivity. However, the legal and regulatory constraints were always there, and the copy went through various tests and filters before it was printed – and it was, as I say, always handled by diligent and responsible sub-editors. Now this process is vanishing.

I suspect that this problem will soon become acute. Perhaps the most vulnerable area of 'traditional' journalism is sports journalism. Roddy Forsyth, my former colleague on the *Sunday Standard*, who is now the Scottish football correspondent for the *Daily Telegraph* and a respected commentator and pundit on BBC Radio Five Live, told me that he was deeply concerned that some younger journalists were over-influenced by the Internet. He said: 'You used to have to cultivate your contacts for information. That was what journalism was all about, contacts. Now some of the younger journalists just trawl through the Internet. What you find there is often a frenzy of misinformation. So, I don't think that's the best basis on which to start. Some of the stuff on the Internet can be quite vindictive.'

I'd emphatically endorse that. I'm not an avid user of the Internet myself; but, as a football fan, I occasionally look for background information on the Net. What I'm likely to find is gossip and innuendo, material that may well have been planted by someone with a commercial or ulterior motive. Print journalists used to have a near-monopoly of newsgathering, which was wrong. And it would be impossibly hypocritical to pretend that you never found gossip, self-serving rumours and innuendo in the mainstream press. But what worries me is that this mainstream press is now itself tempted to source material of dubious provenance on the Internet, and is also trying to compete with it. This is a dangerous and potentially catastrophic nexus.

❝❞

It was early in 2006 that an eight-strong BBC Scotland team, led by series producer Susan Kemp, embarked on an ambitious project to produce six half-hour television programmes about the Scottish press, and particularly its last great glory period. The series was to be transmitted in the autumn of 2006. Susan and her team – the directors Mick Morton and Sharon Adam, the assistant producer Sharon Green, the editor Dave Hipkiss, the researchers Jack McGill and Alan Jones, and the production co-ordinator Ruth Echlin – set about their task with impressive diligence. They interviewed, on film and at considerable length, more than fifty journalists, a few of them still very much involved in producing newspapers, but most of them retired some time ago.

One of their aims was to capture the essence of that rather wild and heady extended Indian summer of print journalism which commenced a few years after the Second World War, when the austerity and the painstaking period of rebuilding and recovery had at last ended. The British people were finally moving on to a new era of hope and plenty after the long years of blood, sacrifice and privation. This was an enormously exciting period for the press, and an era that probably finally ended around the mid-1980s. In retrospect, it was to some extent a period of lost opportunities; but it was overall a glorious time, when circulations were colossal, competition was intense and dirty, even crazy, and the printed newspaper still enjoyed utter primacy in the newsgathering universe. And, here in Scotland, all these factors were intensified, writ even larger. Scotland not only produced several generations of exceptional journalists but was also a nation of confirmed newspaper obsessives, a people who consumed these brittle, absurdly short-lived yet – in their own smudgy way – magical products with a voracious appetite that was unequalled anywhere else.

At the time of writing, well over 100 hours of interviews have been recorded by Susan Kemp and her team, and you don't have to be a genius to work out that very little of this material will actually be shown in the series. I have been privileged to see the transcripts of most of these interviews, and I have been allowed to plunder them freely in the writing of this book. It is almost as if my research has been done for me. I emphasise that this book, strongly subjective and personal as it is, does not seek to mirror the series. But it does, I trust, reflect many of its themes and insights.

And, while I don't want to overstate the importance of these interviews, gathered with commendable industry by the BBC team, I genuinely believe that they represent a collective testimony that has considerable sociological, cultural and historical import. Indeed, I think that the BBC should be persuaded to retain the tapes and perhaps eventually hand them over to a Museum of Scottish Journalism, if such an important institution ever sees the light of day. Certainly, having pondered on the witness and the record of the many interviewees, I have come to the conclusion that such a museum is much needed in Scotland. If the BBC Scotland series *Deadline* indirectly helps to prompt a campaign for such a museum, then well and good.

I was further privileged to spend several days in Glasgow working with the BBC team and hearing their views on this extraordinary world which they were recording, celebrating and – to some extent – analysing. Television journalism is incredibly different from print journalism, and I'd expected that they might have been none too impressed with some of the anecdotes they heard, some of the episodes they unearthed. I was surprised, and rather pleased, to learn that the exact opposite was the case. Towards the end of filming, they seemed to have formed a respect and even an admiration, albeit a qualified admiration, for Scottish print journalism and Scottish journalists.

Here, then, is a digest of the views of Susan's team. Rather than attribute individual quotes, I have mixed them up in a kind of mélange, which I think fairly sums up their considered views as they were completing their long and exhaustive filming of a wide range of interviewees.

'They were surprisingly bright, clever people. They were incredibly open, absolutely candid, up for it and very ready to talk. Yes, many of them could talk for Scotland.' 'There was this constant element of high jinks, as if it was all a game. Yet, underneath, I think they were taking it very seriously indeed.' 'The tabloids and the broadsheets existed in two utterly separate worlds, and it was difficult to find a common denominator. I formed the impression that the broadsheets used to be rather dour, almost Victorian, places to work.' 'It was an incestuous world, but, even so, what came through was this sense of loyalty, total loyalty to the paper they were working on at the time.' 'They were cynical, they were hard-bitten, but they were also quite sentimental, still even today moved by particular stories, all these years on. I'd say a very strong decency came through, and a sense that for them it was much more than just a job.' 'Some of them definitely believed that somehow or other they were giving a voice to the little man.' 'Beneath all the surface cynicism, there is definitely a kind of altruism coming through, and they are actually still really proud of what they were doing.' 'You were conscious that you were recording the passing of an era, and nothing will ever be quite like that ever again.' 'You gained this strong idea that journalists were survivors – papers collapsed, managements crumbled, but the journalists would always move on, would always find another paper.' 'Though they were bitter rivals, looking back they seem to have no sense of animosity at all, they really respected each other.' 'There was an immense pride in their titles, they'd do anything, anything at all, for their papers.' 'There was this meritocracy. People worked their way up and were respected for what they actually did, not for their qualifications. And, of course, some of them had no qualifications.' 'You don't seem to get the drunkenness now – the culture has changed rapidly, out of all recognition.'

'I don't think we should all get too misty-eyed. You could argue that papers are better designed now, they have more pages, more sections, they are clearer, cleaner and are altogether better products.' 'Newspapers may be dying, but not nearly as quickly as some people imagine.' 'I still love the pickupability of the newspaper. You can carry it around with you, read it here, read it there. It isn't dead yet.' 'The newspaper habit remains real, even now, for many people in Scotland.' 'I get three papers a day. Yes, three – my kids laugh at me, though. Yet they do dip into them, and I hope they'll get the newspaper-buying bug eventually.' 'Scotland is a small country, and it's really a pretty tiny constituency for newspapers – but you had this phenomenal range of content, of style, of opinion. They were very distinctive products, very different from each other.' 'There's no way – no way – I'd have wanted to be married to most of these people!' 'Scots tend to be bloody-minded, and, let's face it, these journalists tended to be more bloody-minded than most!' 'All the fun seems to be going out of it now, if it's not already gone. But these folk – they sure had their fun.'

The man in overall charge of the *Deadline* series was the executive producer Neil McDonald, who is Creative Director (Factual) for BBC Scotland. Neil started his career in newspapers, so he had a particular personal interest in the project. He told me, as the series was moving into pre-production: 'The Scottish press holds the mirror up to Scotland and tells us much about ourselves, the people and the country. That's not always a pretty sight, but it is guaranteed to be colourful and vibrant. I've never known an industry peopled by such strong characters. They wouldn't hesitate to sell their granny, but all of them share a love of people and the stories they bring with them that is both invigorating and fulfilling. Before going on to edit television news programmes and documentaries, my own moulding influences came from my newspaper days, and these gave me a respect for facts and for accuracy and also instilled a hunger to find the great tale that sticks with me to this day. The future of the Scottish press, like any other sector of the media, is uncertain, but it's bound to be eventful and exciting. We've been grateful ourselves for the chance to tell something of the story so far.'

The story so far – and of course there's still a long road ahead. What does the future hold? I canvassed the views of four very different commentators: Charles McGhee, Colin McClatchie, Joyce McMillan and Jim Raeburn.

Charles McGhee was appointed editor of the *Herald* early in 2006, after a long stint editing the *Evening Times*. He has a very clear view of the way forward. 'I see my challenge at the *Herald* in three stages. First, to keep the audience that we already have. That is vital. Secondly, to develop it, if at all possible. And thirdly, to gain a new audience through new digital readers. This is crucial. We have to realise that more and more younger readers will be consuming their news online. If we are to survive, it will be through fusing what we do online with what we do in print. Our readers, and more than 80 per cent of them are ABC1, are healthier and wealthier than ever. They still like their news and information in the print format. But, while retaining them – and it's not just a question of retaining them, for I can see at least some growth in this market – we do need more young readers. And probably more female readers too. But the younger market undoubtedly needs a different method of delivery. And I have got to convince my journalists that they have a big future online as well as in print. So, there's a twin approach – our digital edition has to develop alongside our print edition. We are getting to the stage where the online paper experience is pretty close to the print experience. We can now bring the full authority of our brand to our online edition. But I am suggesting that I do need to change the mindset of some journalists and persuade them that the future is a fusion of online and print. I have to break down any sense of demarcation between the two.'

I turned Charles to a consideration of the wider Scottish marketplace. He said: 'Looking back a good few years, it is certainly true that the Scottish press drove the devolution process. Two papers in particular, at different ends of the market: the *Scotsman* for what you might call the chattering classes, and the *Record* for the masses. I worked for the *Record* for eight years, and it is important to recall the backing that the *Record*, a paper with a mass circulation, gave to devolution. It put the populist side of the devolution case. But, since 1997, with New Labour in government and the delivery of constitutional change, we have seen these two papers turning against devolution. We've seen the influence of Martin Clarke, when he was editor at the *Record*, and Andrew Neil as publisher of the *Scotsman*. Two papers that had championed the cause of devolution turned on it almost overnight. After 300 years of not having our Parliament, and after such a vigorous campaign for it, it seemed to me to be a sad time to be a Scottish journalist – two of our leading papers were abandoning their long-standing traditions and beliefs. Looking at the situation now, I believe that it is up to the *Herald* and the *Scotsman* to stand back from the pack and to trust their traditional values. It is still a very competitive marketplace. The English papers that have – for them – relatively small circulations in Scotland, with their Scottish editions, have huge budgets for promotions and marketing. Our task is to convince our readers that Scottish-based and Scottish-produced papers are worth paying a premium price for. There is no doubt that some readers are promiscuous, and a minority will be seduced by promotional offers, by what they see as added value. It is difficult to persuade these readers of the value and importance of the indigenous Scottish product.'

A recurring theme in this book is how the *Record*, for long a venerable and distinguished pan-Scotland tabloid, lost out twice – first to the *Scottish Daily Express*, during a long period of visceral and dirty competition, and more recently to the *Sun*, after a period of only marginally less visceral and dirty competition. During the time that I was writing this book, the *Scottish Sun* was closing in on the *Record*, and may actually have overtaken it. It is, as I write this, slightly premature to pronounce that the *Sun* has definitely triumphed; but it is now clearly winning on the Monday-through-Friday sale, when its price is markedly lower. Saturdays remain a slight problem for the *Sun*, but perhaps not for much longer.

The Murdoch manager who has presided over the *Sun*'s spurt to dominance is Colin McClatchie, who is also quoted elsewhere in this book. A shrewd Northern Irishman, he worked in management roles at both the *Scotsman* and the *Record* before becoming Rupert Murdoch's main man in Scotland in 1995. As I was completing this book, Colin told me: 'It's been a big battle, and it's not over yet. Once we've won – and we are more or less there – we have to sustain it. We can't keep the *Sun*'s price at 10p for ever. So, I'm aware that there's a second battle ahead. I'd say the wider significance of the battle is this. The term "indigenous", which you keep using, Harry, is becoming less and less relevant with each minute that passes. OK, the *Record* was and is an indigenous institution – but let's face it, so was the *Sunday Post*. And look what happened to it. [DC Thomson's *Sunday Post* lost well over a million in its circulation between 1985 and 2005. That, if translated into the industry norm, means well over three million readers.] Everybody in the Scottish press has to understand that it's a completely, totally changing order. It's a genuine mass market now, not simply a Scottish market. All the time, Scotland is becoming more cosmopolitan, more sophisticated.'

I was about to interject that the words 'sophisticated' and *Sun* did not always seem to sit easily together, but Colin anticipated me: 'You watch, Harry. Watch what happens when we start printing the *Times* in Scotland, which we shall be doing from 2007. I think that too many people in the Scottish press believed that the delivery of devolution was going to be some kind of panacea for them, it was going to help them. But it's not worked out like that at all.'

These quotes seem quite aggressive; but, in fairness, I should point out that, while Colin is a very competitive manager, as you would expect of a senior employee of Rupert Murdoch, he has in many ways shown a commitment to Scotland that has been lacking in certain 'now you see them, now you don't' newspaper managers that I could mention. And he has worked immensely hard for the journalists' principal charity, the Newspaper Press Fund. It is not so much that Colin is an enemy of the indigenous – that word again – Scottish press; he is just trying to provide a reality check.

These perspectives are from an editor and a manager. To gain a different – and, as it turned out, more downbeat – overview, I turned to one of Scotland's leading writing journalists, and indeed leading intellectuals, Joyce McMillan. Although her first love is the theatre, and she is probably best known as a theatre critic, Joyce is well established as a trenchant and polemical commentator on Scottish affairs through her work with the BBC and her writing for various papers including the *Herald*, the *Scotsman* and *Scotland on Sunday*. She passionately believes in the necessity of public engagement. She has been chair of the Scottish Civic Forum, and she was a member of the Consultative Steering Group for the Scottish Parliament. A committed trade unionist, she is a long-standing member of the national executive of the National Union of Journalists.

Joyce told me: 'I'm particularly concerned with the arts, and I think the coverage in the Scottish press these days all too often doesn't add much more than you'd get in a London-based paper. A lot of, maybe too much, space goes to writing that is not about the Scottish arts, though I don't want parochialism. Having said that, I think that the coverage of theatre in Scotland is wider and better than it was, say twenty-five years ago. As for news values in the Scottish press, well – I have to say it still seems to be a masculine agenda. It's about conflict, and who's winning, who's losing. There's not too much about, for example, 100,000 people taking peacefully to the streets to demonstrate about world poverty. A few celebrities can trump thousands of ordinary people. More people are now celebrities, for the most slender of reasons, and their influence on the news agenda is greater. There's also this perception – and I think Andrew Neil exemplifies this – of a hostility to Scottish civic society, the civil service, the trade unions and so on.

'A further problem is that the specialists on the papers tend to be ghettoised in special sections and supplements. I know you were a specialist in the 1970s, but at that time you had to fight to get your stories on to the news pages; you rarely had guaranteed space. And people don't look for the media to provide them with information on slow-burn issues. The general presumption seems to be that readers are more interested in crisis, in scandals – and of course in lifestyle. There's a feeling that even the readers of the qualities are not that interested in public affairs. So, I don't think civic Scotland is being at all well covered. There was this tradition in Scottish journalism, until very recently, that it was at least partly about leadership, about leading opinion and asserting agendas. Maybe there was an element of trying to manipulate public opinion, according to the view of the paper; but at least there was confidence that the Scottish press had the ability to change things. There is now a prevalent anti-elitism. Media leadership is seen as elitist.

'And there used to be this demarcation. The tabloid press did the naughty stuff, the quality press did the serious intellectual stuff, and that no longer applies nearly so much. I'd go so far as to say that no longer is there any kind of really close relationship or bond between the Scottish people and their press. There was always a high degree of literacy in Scotland and a very close relationship between Scots and the written word – but we are moving away from that world now. Yet there is still a lingering feeling that newspapers are something that Scots *do*. There remains this general understanding that Scots both create and consume newspapers as few other nations do. That still exists.'

My final pundit was Jim Raeburn, who more than anyone can take a magisterial overview of the Scottish press scene. Jim is both director of the Scottish Newspaper Publishers' Association and director of the Scottish Daily Newspaper Society. He is also on the board of the National Council for the Training of Journalists. Among his many tasks is to act as adviser to the Scottish Editors' Committee – and I have personally benefited from his very shrewd advice as he fulfils this role.

Jim says: 'For very many years, the Scottish papers had the stage more or less to themselves. Now, most of the UK nationals are making a strong effort to penetrate the Scottish marketplace. Look at the *Scottish Sun*, and its battle with the *Record*. Look at the *Sunday Times Scotland*, which sells more than either the *Sunday Herald* or *Scotland on Sunday*. The *Scottish Daily Mail* may have established itself here on the basis of price-cutting, but it has since fully maintained its position in the market. The impact of all this simply has to be negative as far as the indigenous titles are concerned. The national UK titles have very substantial marketing budgets. A few years ago, they suddenly realised it was relatively easy to target Scotland. Some shrewd circulation managers in the south looked at Scotland, and they said: "Look, our figures are far too modest there" – so they invented these Scottish editions, and now they are serious players north of the Border.

'The *Scotsman* and the *Herald* and the *Record* are still genuine Scottish national papers. There is no exact equivalent among the English papers. If you look at the main regional papers in England, their circulations cannot compare with those of the *Herald* and the *Scotsman*, declining as their circulations now are. If you look at titles like the *Yorkshire Post*, the *Northern Echo* or the *Western Daily Press*, their sales are all significantly lower. So, I'd argue firmly that there is still considerable residual strength in our Scottish indigenous dailies. What the Scottish press simply must do is to stabilise the decline. Newspapers are still very profitable operations for the most part. Provided they can continue to win a reasonable share of advertising, the all-important revenue stream should be maintained.

'Newspapers are always under attack, from all sorts of different directions. And yet – publishers are prepared to pay very fancy prices for them. Look at some recent purchases: DC Thomson buying the Aberdeen Journals for £132 million, the Johnston Press buying the Scotsman Group for £160 million, and a couple of years ago Newsquest paying £216 million for the Herald Group. But there is one aspect of our press that does worry me a little, and it is that the quality of writing seems to have deteriorated somewhat. If you look at the *Sunday Standard*, when it appeared twenty-five years ago, there was this quite amazing array of quality writers. But then it was launched at totally the wrong time. Overall, however, I'm certainly not pessimistic.'

‘’

Running through this book has been the story of a race between the *Record* and the *Scottish Sun*. The *Record* has been losing that race, hanging on grimly to an ever-decreasing circulation lead. This battle exemplifies a wider issue: the decline of the indigenous Scottish press and the rise and rise of the so-called tartan editions of the London papers. The process has caused a certain and understandable degree of bitterness. My successor as editor of the *Herald*, Mark Douglas-Home, went so far as to tell me that Scotland was being 'conned' by the London papers with their smattering of Scottish content. 'They've got their readerships here now, but they've absolutely no loyalty to Scotland', he said. 'The indigenous Scottish papers really have to concentrate more on the Scottish Parliament. They cannot mitigate the boredom of much of the Parliament, and at present devolution seems a pretty boring subject, but the Scottish papers simply must try to make it less boring. It's the biggest story they've got.'

It is of course a recurring irony that Scottish devolution – a Herculean constitutional development that was more or less invented and kept burning as an issue by the Scottish press – has, now that it has been achieved, been of so little succour to that press in its time of need. But maybe, as Mark Douglas-Home implies, that is because the Scottish press has to some extent turned on its own creation. Much is made, by me among many others, of the bigger promotional and marketing budgets of the London-based papers. But they have other, more specifically editorial, advantages. A Scottish reader with wide horizons can undoubtedly get a broader range of foreign coverage, and business and arts and sports coverage, in the London-based titles. The obvious way to counter this is by thorough and intelligent and – in a word – unmissable coverage of Scottish affairs.

Everything would change were Scotland to become independent – though, funnily enough, few Scottish papers have ever even begun to take Scottish nationalism seriously. (The *Scottish Sun* attempted to espouse the independence case in 1992, but the tensions between its Scottish edition and the parent edition were such that relatively few people were able to take this particular ploy seriously.) I certainly believe that, during my editorship of the *Herald*, the paper was at least fair and thorough in its treatment of the Scottish National Party; but, as I have shown, even this reasonable and balanced approach provoked fury in some parts of the New Labour machine. And so, one of the more fascinating ongoing plays in the Scottish press will be how the two pan-Scotland quality titles, the *Scotsman* and the *Herald*, belatedly respond to the growing threat from the London titles. As we've seen, Colin McClatchie is very bullish indeed about what the London *Times* will do when it is printed in Scotland in 2007.

One scenario, which I personally would deprecate, is that the *Herald* and the *Scotsman* will retreat into their respective home cities of Glasgow and Edinburgh and become, in essence, city-state newspapers on the US model – upmarket equivalents of the *Press and Journal* in Aberdeen and the *Courier* in Dundee. (Though, having written that, I must in fairness point out that the *P&J*'s circulation area is vast. Even so, it still barely penetrates three of Scotland's four great cities.) Alternatively, the *Herald* and the *Scotsman* could merge. This has been talked about for ages, and I know of at least one proprietor who fairly recently prepared very detailed feasibility plans for a proposed merger. (The obvious business progression would be to merge the advertising and other commercial sides of the two titles, then the printing operations, and finally to combine the two editorial teams.)

Meanwhile, I have perhaps been overdoing the doom and gloom. I should perhaps have made more in this book of two undoubted successes – the new Sunday papers *Scotland on*

Sunday and the *Sunday Herald*, which were launched in 1988 and 1999 respectively. Both quickly established themselves as genuinely pan-Scotland titles, and consolidated strongly. And yet, to echo the themes above, neither manages to beat the circulation of the *Sunday Times Scotland*. Andrew Jaspan, whose talents have unfortunately been lost to the Scottish press, as he is now editing in Australia, was instrumental in the early development of both papers.

Less happy, of course, is the story of the various papers that have fallen by the wayside over the last forty years or so. The *Scottish Daily Express* (though there still exists a much-diluted version of that magnificent paper) was by far the saddest and most spectacular loss. The paper that was set up by some of its staff to replace it, the *Scottish Daily News*, was a short-lived and not particularly heroic failure, tainted by the bombastic interventions of Robert Maxwell. The *Sunday Standard*, a paper of undoubted editorial brilliance, lasted just over two years.

Funnily enough, all three of these failed papers were produced in the 'black Lubyanka' in Albion Street, Glasgow, a building about which I have rhapsodised elsewhere in this book. Perhaps I should have been a little less sentimental. Indeed, maybe there is some kind of curse on the building. That theory is reinforced because yet another failed paper, the *Sunday Scot*, a sketchy tabloid backed by the Rangers owner David Murray, was printed in Albion Street, though its journalists worked elsewhere in Glasgow. It lasted for just four inglorious months in 1991. Surprisingly, since the key editorial instigators of the title were Jack Irvine and Steve Sampson, it was an insipid paper, not especially serious but not particularly raunchy or cheeky either.

And then there was *Business AM*. Launched in Edinburgh by the Bonnier Group in 2000, and an interesting early attempt at the niche or boutique newspaper, it was intended specifically for Scotland's business community. It too failed, not because it lacked quality but because it failed to meet its own (very modest) circulation targets.

( )

We started with the Muppets of Bernie Vickers, a highly successful if wayward editor; we finish with five failed papers. Yes, this chapter has come a long way from its early discussion of the craziness, the clannishness, the mischief and the sentimentality of the Scottish press. It can be a myopic world, the world of Scottish newspapers – but we have, I hope, managed to move seamlessly from recollections of its zanier moments on to a position where a weightier situation report can be presented. In a way, as this chapter journeyed from the absurd to the deeply serious, from the personal and particular to the solemn and the significant, it perhaps somehow mirrored the singular juxtapositions and progressions which are to be found day in, day out, in Scottish newspapers themselves.

10

The Scottish Journalist

A s a youth, I was an eager consumer of newspapers. Bylines were much less common in those days, but those who merited regular bylines tended to be very good writers. Somehow, these names on the printed page indicated people who became friends: writers who were at once distant and proximate. They were remote, faraway figures but also, in a way, good pals. I remember so well being impressed by the sheer grace – the almost poetic quality – of the writing of Cuthbert Graham and John R. Allan in the Saturday edition of the *Press and Journal*. These were journalists of rare class. Many years later, it was a special thrill for me to be able to commission a couple of pieces from Cuthbert Graham, and to interview John R. Allan – possibly the finest writer to have appeared regularly on the pages of a Scottish newspaper in the past fifty years or so. (If I had to choose the best, it would be a stand-off between John R. Allan and the football writer John Rafferty.)

Then there were those who didn't write in anything like so stylish a way, but who also had the status of a friend, because they fought for causes you believed in, or they spoke up for you. They battled for you. One such was Jimmy Forbes, the legendary football writer on the Aberdeen *Evening Express* in the 1960s and 1970s. It was early in the 1960s that, with my customary maladroit timing, I became an avid fan of Aberdeen Football Club at the very time when the Dons were in the doldrums. Jimmy Forbes was a godsend. Fearlessly, and with nit-picking gusto, he attacked the mismanagement and incompetence at the club, and particularly the hapless manager Tommy Pearson and the directors. His thrawn, jagged, constantly angry pieces were a consolatory joy for those who endured too many frustrating and wretched hours on the grim terraces of Pittodrie. A long time later, it was a pleasure for me to make the acquaintance of Jimmy Forbes, a genuine newspaper character if ever there was one, a football writer of the old school, a man with a wonderful, refractory, pawky personality.

In this concluding chapter, I am going to attempt something difficult, and perhaps a little pretentious, and certainly a little sentimental. I am going to essay a composite, a sort of character sketch of the archetypal Scottish journalist.

❛❜

My idea of the Scottish journalist would be a man; there were disgracefully few women working on Scottish newspapers until fairly recently. He would have been born in the early 1920s, so he'd be at his absolute peak in the late 1960s and early 1970s, which was a wonderful time for the Scottish press. He'd have formed a desire to be a journalist at a young age. Maybe he delivered papers in the cold early mornings; maybe one or two papers came into the family home, and he'd heard the stories of the day being discussed by his parents and relatives. Maybe he enjoyed English at school and thought that this was the career most suited to his academic talents, such as they were. Maybe his dad was a reporter, or a printer. Or maybe he'd just seen too many American movies.

He might have been a graduate, but it was more likely that he'd left school at 14 or 15. Maybe he'd started work on a weekly paper, possibly in a tiny newsroom, working with just one or two other tyro reporters, ferreting out the stories in a small Scottish town that was not quite as douce as it seemed on the surface. And maybe he had been lucky in his editor on this weekly, for his boss had become both an informal tutor and something of a father figure. He'd hated his Pitman shorthand lessons, but eventually he'd gained his 100-words-a-minute certificate.

Or maybe he was even more lucky and had found a job in a branch office of one of the big papers; or maybe he was more lucky still, and he'd been a copy boy in one of the main newspaper offices. There he'd be at the beck and call of everyone, and he'd have to get used to being yelled at by sometimes drunk and angry but for the most part warm-hearted journalists, and he'd realise that these journalists came in all shapes and sizes, and from all sorts of backgrounds. If he kept his eyes even half-open, he'd have learned a great deal on each shift. Then the war had intervened, and he might well have seen action in distant places (many of the Scottish journalists I worked with in the 1970s had enjoyed – not perhaps the correct word – eventful wars, though few of them talked much about their experiences).

In the course of his career, he'd have moved from paper to paper once or twice, but not frenetically and frequently as is the case today. He'd be very literate. He'd probably be much more fluent on paper than in speech. Even if he left school at 14, his ability to write lucid, grammatical English quickly and concisely would be well beyond the skills of most of today's young journalists, even if they start with a degree and a postgraduate qualification in journalism. He couldn't touch-type, but he'd taught himself to type, and he could batter out the words at a fair lick. Once or twice, when drunk, he'd got his fingers stuck in the keyboard.

He had an understanding of the world, having knocked about it, and he possessed an eclectic and wide-ranging knowledge – and one of his defining characteristics would be an insatiable curiosity, or, to put it another way, a persistent nosiness. He'd be something of an autodidact. He was, in a quiet, non-political fashion, something of a Scottish patriot. He believed that Scotland was distinctive, and that its press was distinctive. He knew that his country had separate legal, educational and religious traditions that its press had to defend.

He'd have a temper, albeit slow-burning, and he would have a stubborn and sentimental regard for his estate, the fourth and for him the finest, and he would be naturally, effortlessly suspicious of the powerful and the important. He'd be cynical; nothing, but nothing, could surprise him, or so he would claim. That tiresome tyrant the telephone would, in one way or another, play a big part in his life, despite its inconvenience in the days long before mobiles.

He'd love a drink or two or maybe three, and he'd sometimes spend too much time in the pub. He'd prefer drinking with his buddies to chasing women. He'd be a family man, but occasionally he'd find the pull of domesticity less potent than the conviviality of his favourite smoke-filled drinking shop. And yes, he smoked: maybe macho fags like full-strength Capstan, or, if he was a bit of a dandy, a more effete brand like Craven A. He'd be carnaptious but kind, and helpful to his colleagues and friends. But he had a difficult, obstinate, bloody-minded streak.

He could, at times, work with a splendid, almost sublime concentration, doing things with words at speed which relatively few mortals could do. Without notes, he could phone over a complex story from a filthy, vandalised phone box in some desolate, dead-end street. He knew that, at the other end, once his words had left the copytaker, they'd be processed by another man, similar in many respects to himself, a man used to subbing against the clock, a man

190

equally confident with words, who could quickly merge two or three diffuse stories into one readable, clear splash.

He'd not participated in sport since he was relatively young, though he still took an interest, maybe in rugby or golf, but more probably in football or racing. He'd indulge in too many flutters, but his gambling was, like his drinking, just about under control. Whatever his politics, and these were as likely to be on the right as the left, he'd believe in his union, the NUJ, and he'd see it not just as a means of getting the odd large rise or shorter hours (that was a joke) but also as a means of looking after the weaker brethren.

Sometimes he'd be very weary. He'd wonder if it were all worthwhile. He'd seen papers bought and sold, papers close, proprietors come and go, as if newspapers were mere playthings. He'd seen colleagues fired, something that never seemed to happen in other jobs, like teaching. Even if his politics were to the right of centre, he didn't really believe in capitalism, but he knew he was working in a business that was supremely capitalistic, and that he was operating in the most competitive of marketplaces. He knew that nobody, but nobody, owed him a living.

He could not be bothered trying to understand the electronic media, yet he had uneasy intimations that he was already a little out of time. He was suspicious of television, and of television journalists in particular.

But mostly he'd be laughing and bantering. He'd become used to working when others were playing or resting, used to working on Sundays and late into the night. He'd work on public holidays, and on Christmas Day, and he knew that a shift could be shorter or very much longer than was promised. He never ever believed that anything was like it said on the tin.

He'd have encountered rogues and rascals (not all of them his colleagues), he'd have come across some famous people, and he had a good understanding of the fact that most famous people are actually very ordinary. For some reason, the word 'celebrity' was not in his vocabulary.

He knew all too well that, all too often, power is abused. He'd have seen his fellow human beings at their most vulnerable, at their most ridiculous and most stupid. Just occasionally, he sadly concluded that too many people were cretins. At other times, he realised that they could be saints. He had seen people at their happiest. Once or twice, he came across genuine nobility and heroism. And, seeing human beings at their most stressed, at their moments of disaster and triumph, he'd be, without ever admitting it, a bit of a philosopher.

And he sensed that he had been involved in a way of earning a living that was vaguely aberrant. His working life was sometimes dreary and frustrating, sometimes exciting, but hardly ever glamorous, despite the expectations of some of his relatives and his few non-journalistic friends. In his better moments, he'd see this trade – to which, in his way, he'd dedicated his life – as useful and, in its own raffish, slightly shabby fashion, important. When he was in the office and heard the rumble downstairs as the great presses started rolling, he realised that it was, after all, an adventure.

He knew that more lies were written about his trade than he'd ever written himself. Deep down, he knew he was special.

Bibliography

M any books have been written which touch on various aspects of the Scottish press over the past fifty years, but there is a serious need for an encompassing, authoritative, academic history of the modern Scottish press. There are plenty of departments of media studies and Scottish history in Scottish higher education, so there should be many people who are eminently qualified to undertake this important historical and cultural task. I have consulted many books, but I wish to present here only a very exiguous list of those that I have found either particularly useful or particularly enjoyable. I emphasise that this list is about as far from being a definitive catalogue of books about the modern Scottish press as is possible. Many first-class books are not mentioned.

First, I'd like to cite a book that does not, in fact, have that much content about the Scottish press (though what it does say in this context is always pertinent), and that is the superb *The Rise and Fall of the Political Press in Britain* by the US scholar and sometime fellow of All Souls College, Oxford, Professor Stephen Koss. Originally brought out in two volumes, and later condensed into one volume (albeit of almost 1,200 pages), it was first published by Hamish Hamilton in 1981. This is a book of immense and invaluable scholarship. Indeed, it may well be the best book about any aspect of the British media to have been published since 1945. Although urbane and vivid in style, it is an exhaustive study that consistently exudes majestic authority. It is concerned above all with that most crucial of three-way interplays – between journalists, proprietors and politicians.

There are several biographies of the greatest proprietor of them all, Max Aitken, Lord Beaverbrook. I am not sure which is the best, but I am pretty certain that the most enjoyable is the excellent *Beaverbrook: A Life* by Anne Chisholm and Michael Davie (Hutchinson, 1992).

The other books I wish to cite tend to be more anecdotal and subjective in tone. The business journalist Maurice Smith wrote an insightful and instructive survey of the Scottish press called *Paper Lions* (Polygon, 1994), setting himself the task of placing Scottish newspapers in the context of their efforts to maintain the Scottish identity. Jack Webster has written many books; one of the best is his first, *A Grain of Truth* (Paul Harris, 1981). Only a few of the twenty-three chapters deal specifically with the press, but these chapters are especially lively and sharply observed. Murray Ritchie's diary of an important year (1999) in his life as Scottish political editor of the *Herald* is a highly subjective but very perspicacious and revealing – and unfailingly readable – account of a momentous year in Scottish politics (*Scotland Reclaimed*, Saltire Society, 1999).

Then there is Harry Conroy's autobiography *Off the Record* (Argyll Publishing, 1997). This is an enormously gutsy and colourful account of a career that started when Harry was a night messenger on the *Scottish Daily Express*. He progressed, after an eventful interlude as a crime reporter, to being a financial and property specialist on the *Daily Record*. Then he was elected UK leader of the National Union of Journalists. In later life, he was a columnist on the *Herald*, campaign director of the Scottish Constitutional Convention, and finally editor at the *Scottish*

Catholic Observer. His is a racy book, written with terrific gusto. I don't always agree with Harry's perspectives on controversial issues, but there can be no doubting his effervescent commitment to journalism, to Christian socialism and to Scotland. There will be more magisterial books on aspects of the Scottish press, but few that are as much fun.

There are many novels about journalism, not least because so many journalists have gone on to become novelists. In my opinion, the best is by that underrated and boisterous novelist, Gordon M. Williams: *The Upper Pleasure Garden* (Hodder & Stoughton, 1970). It is not set in Scotland, but it is a whirlwind of a read. Williams, the son of a policeman from a tough area of Paisley, wrote many pugnacious and vital novels in the 1960s and 1970s. It is high time he was rediscovered.

6 9

I have asked, while writing this book, a selection of interested parties to name the man or woman whom they regarded as the finest Scottish journalist of the twentieth century. I emphasise that the results of this wholly informal and subjective survey, based on a small and no doubt idiosyncratic sample of opinion, should not be taken too seriously.

Anyway, the man who emerged in third place was Eric Mackay, the Aberdonian who edited the *Scotsman* with distinction between 1972 and 1985. In second place came Ian McColl, a typical Beaverbrook senior employee in that he had a 'good' war in the RAF and was a strict Presbyterian. He served for twenty years as session clerk of the Sandyford Henderson Memorial Kirk in the west end of Glasgow. McColl also worked tirelessly for the journalists' charity, the Newspaper Press Fund. He edited the *Scottish Daily*

Express from 1961 to 1971 and the *Daily Express* in London from 1971 to 1974, and in my experience he is spoken of with more affection and respect than any other modern Scottish journalist.

Both Mackay and McColl were essentially production journalists who wrote hardly anything; the man who came first in my mini-poll maybe wrote too much. He was James Cameron, a prolific – probably too prolific, his output was uneven – foreign correspondent and sometime historian. He was Scottish through and through, though he was actually born in Battersea, London, in 1911. He served a long apprenticeship as a sub-editor, working first for DC Thomson in Dundee and Glasgow, and then for the *Scottish Daily Express* in Albion Street, Glasgow. He went on to become widely regarded as the greatest of all British foreign correspondents in the twentieth century. (Incidentally, his relationship with his proprietor Lord Beaverbrook was extremely volatile.)

Cameron's autobiography, *Points of Departure*, was published in 1967 by Arthur Barker. It does not have that much to say about the Scottish press. It is very wordy, and in truth a little disappointing; Cameron himself insisted on the subtitle *An Experiment in Autobiography*. Yet it contains several spellbinding passages, and for these it deserves to be read by anyone interested in twentieth-century journalism.

Acknowledgements

I am grateful to Neil McDonald, executive producer, and Susan Kemp, series producer, who led the team that created the BBC Scotland television series *Deadline*. Without them, this book would never have existed. I also wish to thank the members of that team, Mick Morton, Sharon Adam, Sharon Green, Dave Hipkiss, Jack McGill, Alan Jones and Ruth Echlin, for their stimulating insights and comments. As outsiders who suddenly became involved in the crazy and somewhat self-regarding world of the Scottish press, they have taken a generously benign and positive view of it all.

I also wish to thank the many journalists who have helped me. Not all journalists are great talkers – but, my goodness, the BBC team tracked down those who were as fluent in the spoken word as on paper. Older, retired journalists can have the time and inclination to talk until the cows come home; but their anecdotes are often wonderful, and their witness is significant in a sociological and cultural sense. In a way, I am even more grateful to those journalists still involved in the daily grind who spoke to me, because their time is more precious, and they do not have the languid luxury of looking back contentedly in the direction of a golden era. Well, it was a golden era; but that does not make things any easier for those struggling manfully with the challenges of the present.

In some ways, it is invidious to name individuals, since so many have helped me; but I must mention Jim Raeburn, who will retire in 2007 from his various posts and who will be an immeasurable loss to Scottish print journalism. Jim knows more about the industry, in an objective, dispassionate way, than anyone else around. I thank him for his counsel, always given unstintingly and willingly. I am also grateful to Andrew Hood for talking me, patiently and carefully, through the genesis of the *Scotsman's* long and remarkable campaign for Scottish devolution.

I'd like to thank my wife, Julie Davidson, to whom I owe rather more than I am sometimes prepared to admit. In this context, I wish to thank her not just for telling me her own tales and anecdotes, but also for listening with patience over the years as I subjected her to all of mine. In particular, she has helped me to understand, if imperfectly, what it was like to be a woman in the macho, bruising world of Scottish newspapers thirty and forty years ago.

Finally, I wish to thank Ann Crawford, head of Saint Andrew Press, for her continuing support and unremitting professionalism. I am also most grateful to her colleagues Richard Allen and Ivor Normand.

Index

Index

Index

Index